TWAYNE'S WORLD AUTHORS SERIES
A Survey of the World's Literature

Sylvia E. Bowman, Indiana University
GENERAL EDITOR

FRANCE

Maxwell A. Smith, Guerry Professor of French, Emeritus
The University of Chattanooga
Former Visiting Professor in Modern Languages
The Florida State University

EDITOR

Xavier de Maistre

TWAS 447

Xavier de Maistre

XAVIER DE MAISTRE

By CHARLES M. LOMBARD
University of Illinois

TWAYNE PUBLISHERS
A DIVISION OF G. K. HALL & CO., BOSTON

Library of Congress Cataloging in Publication Data

Lombard, Charles M.
  Xavier de Maistre.

  (Twayne's world authors series ; TWAS 447 ; France)
  Bibliography: p. 153 - 54.
  Includes index.
  1. Maistre, Xavier, comte de, 1763 - 1852.
2. Authors, French—19th century—Biography.
PQ2342.M3Z77   843'.6   76-58855
ISBN 0-8057-6284-1

Contents

About the Author

Charles M. Lombard is Professor of French at the University of Illinois, Chicago Circle. A specialist in Franco-American literary relations during the Romantic period, he is the author of *French Romanticism on the Frontier* (Madrid: Editorial Gredos).

Professor Lombard's additional publications include the Twayne's World Authors Series volume *Lamartine* (TWAS 254, 1973), a study of the French Romantic poet who also played an important political role; and *Joseph de Maistre* (TWAS 407, 1976), an effort to focus on the literary contributions of that controversial figure. Xavier de Maistre, Joseph's younger brother and also a popular writer in the period of French Romanticism, is the subject of Professor Lombard's latest TWAS publication.

Presently in press is Professor Lombard's *Thomas Holley Chivers*, a study of the cantankerous contemporary of Edgar Allan Poe, prepared for Twayne's United States Authors Series

Preface

At one time in the nineteenth century Xavier de Maistre's *Voyage autour de ma chambre* was widely read in Europe and America. The number of editions of his works in French and in translation attests to the popularity of his four other tales. Generally forgotten today, he is remembered only on occasion, in association with his brother, Joseph de Maistre, well known as a polemicist, political philosopher, and creative writer.

Five tales, a limited production, would seem to justify Xavier's oblivion. Such is not the case. In his day he was recognized as a charming and innovative writer and the only French author to compose a successful work patterned after Laurence Sterne's *Sentimental Journey* with verve and originality. Another little known and unappreciated contribution made by Xavier is his treatment of Russian subjects.

The present study proposes to analyze Xavier's five tales in depth in order to determine their significance not only in relation to their own time, but their relevance to the current literary scene. Xavier's role as precursor will be examined with the aim of clarifying his contributions to short fiction in technique, structure, and subject matter. In addition, a fragment of a projected prose work will be studied to ascertain the probable directions of his further efforts in literature if he had continued to write. His poetry will also be discussed, particularly his renditions of the verse fables of Krylov, the noted Russian fabulist. Xavier's correspondence will not be treated owing to limitations of space. Points, obvious to specialists, will be explained for the benefit of students and general readers. It is hoped that readers will acquire a better understanding of a neglected but important figure in nineteenth century French literature.

Chronology

1763   November 8: birth of Xavier de Maistre at Chambéry.

1774   July 21: death of Christine de Maistre, Xavier's mother.

1781   June 13: Xavier enlists in the Regiment de la Marine.

1784   Publication of *Les Premiers essais de Xavier de Maistre*.

1784   April 22: failure of Xavier's first balloon ascension.
May 5: second ascension succeeds.

1789   January 15: death of Xavier's father.

1790   January-February: Xavier duels with Patono de Méiran, and afterwards is confined to quarters where he composes *Voyage autour de ma chambre*.

1791   March 25: leaves Turin for garrison duty at Fénestrelle.

1792-
1798   Period of Xavier's sojourn in Aosta.

1794   *Voyage autour de ma chambre* published in Turin.
February 3: Marie-Dauphine (Élisa) marries Jean-Joseph Barrillier.

1795   In early spring Xavier reads *Voyage autour de ma chambre* in Lausanne at salon of Mme Hüber Alléon.

1796   April 28: Napoleon forces king of Sardinia to sign an armistice.

1799   April 14: Marshal Suvarov chases French out of Italy.
October 4: Xavier leaves Italy to join Russian army in Switzerland.

1800   January 26: Xavier leaves for Russia.
March 1: Xavier enters czar's service.

1803   May 13: Joseph takes up residence in Saint Petersburg as Sardinian ambassador to czar's court.

1805   March 16: Xavier is named director of the Department of the Admiralty.

1807   December 12: Xavier is made lieutenant-colonel in Russian forces.

1809   August 26: Xavier is promoted to the rank of colonel.

1810   July 9: Xavier leaves Saint Petersburg to join Russian army in Georgia.

November 22: Xavier is wounded in action against the Turks.

1811   *Le Lépreux de la cité d'Aoste* appears in Saint Petersburg without mention of the author.

1813   February 3: Xavier weds Sophie Zagriatsky.

July 18: Xavier is made major-general.

1814   November 28: birth of Xavier's daughter, Alexandrine.

1815   *Les Prisonniers du Caucase* and *La Jeune Sibérienne* are published at Paris by Dondey-Dupré and Ponthieu.

1816   Xavier resigns from Russian army.

1817   May 27: Joseph bids his last farewell to Xavier and returns to Savoy.

1820   February 21: death of Xavier's son, André.

1824   An edition of *Le Lépreux de la cité d'Aoste*, attributed to Joseph de Maistre, is published by Gosselin in Paris.

1825   *Expédition nocturne autour de ma chambre* is published in Paris by Dondey-Dupré and Ponthieu.

1826   October: Xavier returns to Sardinia and visits Turin.

1827   March 10: Xavier visits Rome.

1837   October 13: death of Xavier's son, Arthur.

1838   July: Xavier leaves Italy.

October: Xavier visits Lamartine at Saint-Point.

November 6: Xavier arrives at Paris where he meets Sainte-Beuve and other literary figures.

1839   April: Xavier leaves Paris to return to Russia.

May: Sainte-Beuve publishes sketch of Xavier in *Revue des deux mondes* which offends the latter.

July: Xavier arrives in Russia after an absence of twelve years.

1841   December 9: death of Élisa at Aosta.

1842   July 7: Xavier complains to a friend about Sainte-Beuve's biographical sketch of him.

1844   April 30: Xavier learns of the death of Louis de Vignet, his nephew and the brother-in-law of Lamartine.

1851   August 30: death of Xavier's wife.

1852   June 13: Xavier dies in Strelne at the home of Mme Lanskoï.

CHAPTER 1

Biographical Sketch and Early Works

I Early Years

XAVIER de Maistre was born at Chambéry at the Hôtel de Salins on November 8, 1763. The Maistre family was originally from Languedoc and subsequently went to Italy, residing first in Nice and eventually settling in Savoy. Xavier's father was made a count in 1780 by the king of Sardinia in recognition of his services to the crown as a magistrate. Rough and provincial in manner, Count François-Xavier was at heart a warm and sensitive person, a quality he imparted to his two literary sons, Joseph and Xavier. Their mother, Christine Desmotz, had married François-Xavier in 1750, when she was only twenty-three and her husband's junior by twenty-two years. There were fifteen children in all, five of whom died at an early age. Joseph, future author of *Du Pape* and the *Soirées de Saint-Pétersbourg*, was ten years older than Xavier. A bond was formed between the two brothers that grew stronger with the development of their mutual literary interests. Their mother read aloud to them from the great works of French Classicism and encouraged their natural creative talents. Deeply religious, she left to both sons a lasting impression of the faith and piety inspired in her by Catholicism. Although their father has at times been compared to the father of Chateaubriand, he was not quite so somber and solemn and, judging from Xavier's recollections, much more approachable.[1]

Xavier differed from Joseph in many ways. Of somewhat delicate health, he was in temperament what the Savoyards called a *baban*, a carefree, absent-minded loafer, by no means the most promising pupil for a rigorous teacher. Fortunately the family made a good decision by placing Xavier in the hands of an understanding priest at La Bauche. Allowed to progress at his own pace, Xavier acquired a lively interest in science, languages, music, painting, and

11

literature. The kind-hearted cleric in charge of Xavier's education was the Abbé André Isnard, who, while essentially orthodox in matters pertaining to Catholic theology, was highly unconventional when it came to instructing the *baban*. Xavier was fortunate in being entrusted to a sympathetic individual who allowed him free rein in self-expression and in molding his own tastes. The relationship between Xavier and Abbé Isnard was akin to that of Émile and the Vicaire Savoyard, although perhaps not quite so radical in every respect as the teacher-pupil association outlined by Rousseau. In such relaxed surroundings the future writer and painter developed his talents. His period of education under Abbé Isnard was saddened on July 21, 1774, by the death of his mother, who had traveled to La Bauche to visit Xavier there.

By the time he was eighteen Xavier was a robust teenager ready to join the Sardinian army, which had a peacetime quota of 30,000 and numbered 45,000 when on a war footing. On June 13, 1781 he enlisted as a volunteer in the Regiment of the Marine. At that moment the Savoyards and the Piedmontese, especially in the Sardinian forces, had a reputation as fierce and formidable soldiers. Their only complaint was the boredom of army life when the nation was at peace. The regimen of military service had a stabilizing effect on the impulsive *baban*, who became conscientious and punctilious in the performance of his duties. He still found the time to read, socialize, and to entertain such fantasies as the construction of wings for a flight to America and the unwarlike project of writing a novel.

II   *Balloon Ascensions, Romance, and Campaigns*

The year 1784 was an eventful one in Xavier's career when he became involved in balloon ascensions. The Montgolfier brothers had launched the first balloon a year before, and Pilatre de Rozier was engaged in aeronautical experiments that eventually cost him his life. Consequently, the aristocracy of Savoy was anxious to underwrite a balloon launching by some intrepid Savoyards. A public subscription raised the necessary funds, and the services of Xavier, already interested in physics and chemistry, were acquired. The balloon was spherical in shape, thus presumably making it easier to navigate. There was some class struggle over the credit to be assigned for initiating the experiment in air travel on Sardinian soil. Some merchants, members of the bourgeoisie and resentful of aristocratic airs, composed a satirical poem on the forthcoming event denouncing the nobility for taking all the credit: "One will have burned, for good reason, the titles of each house. And from these ignited charters the smoke will be preserved to fill all this taffeta and to take the place of gas. . . ."[2]

Entitled the *Voyage du Casin*, that is, a trip of the circle of nobility, the poem already foreshadowed the spirit of the French Revolution. This display of class prejudice did not undermine the efforts to send the balloon aloft. On April 22, 1784, at eleven o'clock, a first launching was attempted, but the balloon tipped over and flapped helplessly on the ground. Another outpouring of satirical poetry by local wags ridiculed the futile venture. Xavier and his fellow aeronaut, Louis Brun, were not discouraged. Additional funds were collected to repair the damaged balloon and a second ascension at six o'clock on the morning of May 5, two weeks later, succeeded. As the vehicle mounted into the air, Xavier's comrades in the Regiment of the Marine were marching below and cheered the successful launching. The balloon attained a height of 2,000 meters and the two occupants enjoyed a good view of the countryside. They landed at the same site from which they ascended, the Park of Buisson-Rond, and were greeted by the populace and many celebrities of the Sardinian court. A banquet was held that night in honor of Xavier and Louis Brun. In 1784 Xavier wrote a short tract recounting his impressions of the successful balloon ascension on May 5, the *Lettre le de Comte de C.*** off *** dans l'*** des C*** contenant une relation de l'expérience aérostatique de Chambéry.*

While on garrison duty in 1785 - 86, first at Exilles and then at Pignerol, he planned on writing a novel, the *Prisonnière de Pignerol,* but it was never completed. He read widely in the literature popular at the time: Macpherson's questionable version of the Gaelic bard, Ossian, the *Night Thoughts* of Young, the *philosophes;* and undoubtedly Cervantes, Ariosto, and Shakespeare. There was considerable rivalry in the ranks between the French-speaking Savoyards and the Italian Piedmontese. The men from Savoy, while loyal to an Italian king, resented any slurs against the culture of France. Xavier was intensely nationalistic in a cultural sense and in all probability crossed swords more than once with young hotheads from Piedmont. The one recorded duel of significance took place in Turin, where Xavier was then stationed, on the eve of the carnival season in January or February of 1790. His opponent was a notorious brawler, Patono de Meïran, and,

more than likely, the usual insults between Savoyards and Piedmontese led to an armed clash. Evidently Xavier wounded Patono
and emerged the victor at the expense of a few scratches inflicted by
his adversary's blade.

Confined to his quarters for forty-two days, Xavier was unexpectedly started off on his literary career. It is quite possible that he
already had a rough draft of the *Voyage autour de ma chambre*, but
the house arrest obliged him to think seriously of completing it.
Laurence Sterne's *Sentimental Journey* and *Tristram Shandy* had
substantial influence on Xavier's work, along with other master-
pieces of European literature. Four years later Xavier took the
manuscript with him to Switzerland when he visited Joseph in
Lausanne. The older brother made a few corrections and, to
Xavier's delight, the *Voyage autour de ma chambre* was published
in April 1795. In the following year a second edition appeared in
Paris. Encouraged by favorable reviews of the *Voyage* Xavier
thought seriously of an immediate sequel but was dissuaded by
Joseph.

With the outbreak of war in Italy, and the invasion of Sardinia in
1792 by revolutionary troops from France, the Sardinian king was
dethroned and many of the nobles were driven into exile. Xavier
had advanced rapidly since he first joined the Regiment of the
Marine. At twenty-four, in 1787, he was promoted to the rank of
adjutant-major, and prior to the outbreak of hostilities he had enjoyed the carefree social life of a young officer. A witty conver-
sationalist, he had free entry to the salons of any city where he was
stationed and ample leisure to carry on his artistic and scientific
pursuits. Additional promotions, to the rank of lieutenant on
September 24, 1790, and to that of lieutenant adjutant-major on
February 12, 1794, reflected the extent of his adaptation to a
military career. Warfare in the 1790s was still waged in the manner
long characteristic of European campaigns. During the winter the
French and the Sardinians, with their Austrian allies, kept at a
respectful distance from one another with no major battles and only
a few minor skirmishes. Xavier did participate in hard-fought conflicts throughout 1795 and 1796. Now a captain as of January 20,
1795, he continued to serve his king until Napoleon forced Victor-
Amédée III to sign an armistice on April 28, 1796. The weary
monarch died the same year, October 16, 1796, and was succeeded
by his son, Charles-Emmanuel IV. Two years later the newly crowned king was obliged, in the face of armed revolution in Piedmont

and at the behest of the French occupation troops, to abdicate, on December 9, 1798.

From 1792 - 1798 Xavier was assigned to Aosta, an ancient city in Piedmont in the province of Turin, dating from Roman times. Little did he suspect that Aosta was to provide the setting for *Le Lépreux de la Cité d'Aoste*. In the city was located the Tour de la Frayeur, the residence of a leper, Pierre-Bernard Guasco, whose entire family the parents and eight children, was afflicted with the dread malady. In June 1773, Victor-Amédée III sent the survivors, the father and three children, to Aosta for care and treatment. Pierre-Bernard's sister, Marie-Lucie Ange, to whom he was deeply attached, passed away on September 3, 1791, at the age of thirty-two. Pierre lived in solitude for three years after her death, until Xavier came to Aosta and began to pay the leper periodic visits. The main outlines of Xavier's work represent a reasonably accurate account of Pierre's circumstances and the author's contact with him. Even the dog, Miracle, described by Xavier, actually existed; the dirty grayish mongrel was a source of comfort to the poor leper. Pierre-Bernard Guasco, a devout Catholic, died on December 13, 1803, completely unaware that he would be known to posterity through *Le Lépreux de la Cité d'Aoste*.

Among the details faithfully recorded by Xavier concerning the occupant of the Tour de la Frayeur was the presence of two lovers who often met near the tower. The two persons, whose happiness aroused the envy of the leper watching them in frustrated silence, were Marie-Dauphine Ubertin and Jean-Joseph Barrillier, royal notary and officer in the militia. Xavier in his description of Guasco was sufficiently realistic, but eliminated the more gruesome aspects of the leper's disfigured body and the psychological trauma experienced by Pierre-Bernard. On his visits to the tower Xavier was not always alone. Frequently he was accompanied by a local belle, Marie-Dauphine, the widow of Jean-Joseph Barillier. The lovers, so envied by Guasco, had only a short period of happiness, the husband having died in 1795. Xavier had loved Marie-Dauphine for several years and prior to her marriage sought her hand in vain. His hopes were renewed now that she was a widow, and their relationship soon blossomed into a promising romance. She called him "Joris," and his term of affection for her was "Élisa"; Xavier refers to her by this name in the *Expédition nocturne*. Not long after the death of M. Barillier, Xavier courted Élisa and sometime in August of 1797 his sister Jeanne (Jenny) was writing to their brother, Nicolas, about the prospective addition to the Maistre family; Jenny judged Élisa to be pretty, although otherwise quite commonplace in speech and manner.

Family disapproval is an age-old stumbling block to lovers bent on getting married, but in Xavier's case other factors probably intervened. With the defeat of the Sardinian cause at the hands of Napoleon, Xavier was stripped of title and income. Élisa might well have had second thoughts about a marriage with such an uncertain future. She may also have sensed some opposition and resentment in Xavier's family. At any rate, the wedding was called off, and shortly after Xavier's departure for Russia in 1800 Élisa married M. Decoularé, a French officer. Over twenty-five years later their friendship was to be renewed.

III   Career in Russian Service

Downcast at Élisa's rejection and temporarily disillusioned by the abdication of Charles-Emmanuel IV, Xavier returned to Turin in 1799 and took up residence in a fifth floor flat of a building on the Rue de la Providence, the locale of the *Expédition nocturne autour de ma chambre*, to be published years later as a sequel to the popular *Voyage*. Official Sardinian military records indicate that, for all practical purposes, after December 17, 1798, Xavier de Maistre was no longer a member of the army. This did not mean, however, that he had put up the sword never to fight Napoleon — far from it; the battle had only begun. The Russian commander, Marshal Alexander Suvarov, obliged the French to retreat and occupied Turin. Charles-Emmanuel IV was restored to the throne by Suvarov, but Austrian intrigue forced Czar Paul I to withdraw support of the Sardinian king and to recognize instead Austria's claim to Savoy and Piedmont. Xavier shared Suvarov's contempt for the Austrians and, deciding to serve Russia rather than Austria, on October 3, 1799 joined the Russian army when it marched into Switzerland. The next day, without permission from his superiors in the Sardinian army, he left Turin. Although Xavier wished to retain his captaincy in the Sardinian forces, the record of his departure to serve the czar was sufficiently unclarified to warrant charges later by enemies that he had deserted. The campaign in Switzerland was not overly rigorous and Xavier found the time to paint several portraits, among them those of Suvarov and Charles-Emmanuel IV. In January 1800 Czar Paul I, discouraged by Russian reverses, ordered the troops to return home. Xavier accompanied Suvarov back to Russia and counted on the marshal's influence to embark on a fresh career there. His hopes were short-lived. The mercurial czar turned against Suvarov, and the crestfallen marshal died in Xavier's arms May 18, 1800.

In Saint Petersburg Xavier was faced with the immediate task of making a living. He kept the title of captain in order to have some status in Russian society. Prospects for employment were delayed by the assassination of Paul I March 23, 1801; and thrown on his own resources, Xavier turned to painting. He left Saint Petersburg September 26, 1801, to establish himself as a painter in Moscow. Fortunately he obtained the patronage of Princess Anna Petrowna Schakowskoï, who sent clients to him in a pleasant studio where he painted portraits. The princess' generosity moved her to invite Xavier to reside in her home indefinitely as a guest; and thus Xavier spent many a pleasant evening in the company of Princess Schakowskoï and her family. Careful to leave all doors open to future career opportunities in Russia, Xavier obtained permission to retire from active service in the czar's army, but retained the rank of major and the right to wear the uniform. Painting was an uncertain profession in Russia where, during the winter months, there were only three hours of daylight and considerable competition from other painters.

After three years in Russia, Xavier was overjoyed by the arrival in Saint Petersburg on May 13, 1803, of his brother Joseph, the newly appointed Sardinian minister to Russia on behalf of Victor-Emmanuel I (Charles-Emmanuel IV having abdicated in favor of his brother). Joseph, to his surprise, learned that Xavier managed to support with his brush their sister Thérèse and their brother Abbé André, also exiled in Russia. Contrary to some versions to the effect that Joseph talked Xavier into abandoning painting for an office more becoming to an ambassador's brother, it was Xavier who volunteered to take the step, although the latter's career as a painter was slowly improving at Moscow where Xavier was a guest in the salon of Serge Pushkin. There Xavier met the host's little boy Sacha, the future Alexander Pushkin.

Joseph lost no time in procuring a position for Xavier, through the intercession of the influential Admiral Tchitchagof, director of the Department of the Admiralty; Xavier's duties included the supervision of a new library. The elder Maistre announced the good news to Xavier March 16, 1805. The irony of the situation was that the younger brother enjoyed a life of comparative luxury while the unhappy Joseph subsisted on a meager salary from his exiled monarch. In fact, he was reduced to eating bread and water for breakfast in order to be able to afford the footman and coach necessary for a foreign minister in the czar's court.

Xavier assumed the duties of his new office in Moscow in 1805. Other Sardinian émigrés there were jealous of his progress, and when he attained the rank of lieutenant-colonel in 1807 their fury knew no bounds; he already held the title of count. Rumors were spread about his deserting the Sardinian army, but to no avail. Joseph had powerful friends at the Russian court and, moreover, events in Europe in 1807 absorbed everyone's attention. Russia had made peace with France, and Joseph was thinking seriously of asking Napoleon to restore Sardinian independence now that the czar showed little interest in Sardinia. Diplomacy did not constantly occupy Joseph's mind; the formidable author of the *Soirées* more than once broached the subject of religion with Xavier. Displeased with the latter's laxity in spiritual matters, Joseph most likely told him to read a well-known Savoyard author, St. Francis de Sales. Xavier evidently took Joseph's advice to heart for by 1809 he was again attending mass regularly.

Changes of administrative heads at the Russian court did not affect Xavier. When Admiral Tchitchagof was replaced by the Marquis de Traversay, a former officer in the French navy, Xavier continued to advance in rank and was named colonel August 26, 1809. Enemies in Sardinian émigré circles once more calumniated their successful countryman; Xavier was too busy to bother about such pettiness. *Le Lépreux de la Cité d'Aoste* occupied much of his spare time in 1810 and he also worried about the possibility that the Department of the Admiralty would be abolished and with it his lucrative position. Restored to active duty in the Russian army, he left Saint Petersburg July 9, 1810, to join the troops in Georgia. Wounded in the right arm during a fierce encounter with the Turks in November, he recuperated and began to collect material for two more tales, *Les Prisonniers du Caucase* and *La Jeune Sibérienne*. In the period of convalescence he had the opportunity to study the wild tribes in Georgia and to make perceptive observations on Russian customs and life. Unlike Joseph, who could scarcely utter two words in Russian, Xavier mastered the language. It was an accomplishment that stood him in good stead when he courted Sophie Zagriatsky, an in-law of the poet Pushkin. They became engaged in

1811. Plans for the wedding were interrupted by Napoleon's invasion of Russia in 1812. With the defeat of Bonaparte, Xavier, who served with distinction in the czar's army during the campaign, was able to proceed with arrangements for the marriage, which took place on February 3, 1813. He served three more years in the Russian army and in 1816 retired to live peacefully and raise a family in Saint Petersburg. Xavier had taken his time to renounce celibacy, being married when he reached the age of fifty. Thanks to his wife's personal fortune the family was financially secure.

IV *Return to Savoy*

When Joseph left Saint-Petersburg in 1817 to return to Savoy, it proved to be the brothers' final farewell, for Joseph died in Chambéry four years later. Xavier was further saddened by the death of two of his four children, Alexandrine and André. Concerned about the health of his remaining son and daughter, he gave serious consideration to a trip to the warmer climate of Italy. The demands of a literary career caused a slight delay in his plans; it was necessary to arrange for the publication in Paris in 1825 of a definitive edition of his tales, to which two fresh titles were added, *Les Prisonniers du Caucase* and *La Jeune Sibérienne.*

Alarmed by the weakened condition of his son and daughter, Xavier departed for Italy in 1826. He returned to his native land a wealthy aristocrat, in sharp contrast with his departure years before as an impoverished soldier. Xavier spent almost twelve years in Italy, largely in the vicinity of Pisa, Naples, and Rome. Catherine and Arthur, his two remaining children, died in that period. A brother, Nicolas, and a sister, Theresine, also passed away. Although grief-stricken by these untimely deaths, Xavier still profited by his sojourn in Italy, indulging his intellectual interests and maintaining a lively correspondence with Lamartine, Sainte-Beuve, and other writers.

After the demise of his son in 1838, Xavier decided to return to Russia, but stopped off on the way to see Paris. It was his first visit to France and Paris surprised him a good deal. Romantic mannerisms and religious indifference must have shocked the seventy-five year old gentleman, now a confirmed reactionary and no longer the rambunctious author of the *Voyage autour de ma chambre.* Nonetheless he was deeply touched by the warm reception accorded him and the tributes paid to his work.

V   *Return to Russia and Final Years*

After an absence of twelve years, Xavier returned to Russia in July 1839. His family ties there had linked him with Russia's outstanding national poet, Alexander Pushkin. The celebrated writer became Xavier's nephew-in-law, so to speak, when he married Nathalie Gontcharova, niece of Xavier's wife. Pushkin had met Xavier in Saint Petersburg when he was only six, and their association doubtless served to fix more firmly in the mind of the future poet the importance of French culture; any influence, of course, was only general in nature, since Pushkin later discovered his own national roots and acquired a great love for the Russian language. Xavier referred to his nephew-in-law as the great poet and once attempted a translation of a few passages from Pushkin's writings; he soon destroyed the translation, probably realizing that an adequate rendering of Pushkin in French was a formidable task. The Russian poet, after acquiring a substantial reputation in literary circles, became in 1832 the object of constant surveillance by the czar's police, apprehensive about his liberal ideas; in 1837 he was killed in a duel when defending his wife's honor. They had become the center of intrigue in Moscow society. Xavier was shocked by Alexander's death, but his sympathies were definitely with Mme Pushkin: "One cannot reproach the poor widow, all of whose misfortune came from being too beautiful and too sought after. The husband was *a hot head,* his adversary *a bad character;* no one was really in love; vanity wounded everyone."[3]

Xavier's wife was distressed by the news of Pushkin's death, since she was very fond of her niece Nathalie. When the Maistres returned to Russia, Mme Pushkin lived with them temporarily, along with her four children; she soon departed, after marrying a Russian officer, Colonel Lanskoï, but left the Maistres with pleasant memories of her stay. Xavier welcomed her presence: "On the first floor another niece will be living, Mme Pushkin, widow of the famous poet killed in a duel, about whom you have undoubtedly heard, with one of her sisters and four children; she is very beautiful and a very fine person."[4]

The unfortunate duel involved the Maistre family in more ways than one. A French émigré, Georges d'Anthès, the "bad character" who killed the poet, was the husband of another of Mme de Maistre's nieces, a sister of Mme Pushkin. Xavier's opinion of Anthès was shared by most Russians.

In May 1852 he wrote one of his last letters to a niece, Mlle Olympe de Vignet, in which he seemed to sense that the end was near: "I have absolutely lost my memory. . . . I beseech you to tell my friends that I will not write to them anymore, but that I always love them with all my heart."[5]

During the early part of June of the same year, Pushkin's widow, now Mme Lanskoï, invited Xavier to her country home at Strelne. Delighted to accept the invitation, he went there prepared to write another tale along lines similar to *Les Prisonniers du Caucase* and *La Jeune Sibérienne*. Shortly after his arrival at Mme Lanskoï's he fell ill, and early on the morning of June 13, 1852, died in his sleep. Père Jacques Skiliondz, a Dominican, officiated at the funeral. Xavier was buried in Saint Petersburg in the Smolensk Cemetery in a plot assigned there to Roman Catholics.

With a good-natured fatalism he had prepared, long before his demise, his own epitaph with a dash and flavor somewhat reminiscent of La Fontaine: "Here lies under this gray stone *Monsieur Bans* who was surprised by everything, asking where the north wind came from and why Jupiter thundered. He studied many an obscure book, read from morning to night, and finally drank the dark waters, very surprised at learning nothing."[6]

Much of the carefree spirit witnessed years earlier in the *Voyage autour de ma chambre* entered into the composition of the merry and death-defying epitaph. The likable Xavier de Maistre, sincere to the end and never once mistaken about the importance of his limited but meaningful literary works, died on foreign soil, far from the native Savoy he cherished and from France, his cultural homeland.

CHAPTER 2

Voyage autour de ma Chambre

I *Background and Summary*

XAVIER composed the *Voyage autour de ma Chambre* while confined to quarters after a duel in the winter of 1790. On a visit to Lausanne in the spring of 1795, he read the manuscript to friends at the salon of Mme Hüber Alléon. The work was finally published in Turin in 1794.

The *Voyage*, as the title indicates, is an imaginary trip around Xavier's room, during a period of house arrest. Readers are introduced to Joannetti, the valet, and Rosine, Xavier's dog. The tone of the essay varies from the frivolous to the profound, with speculations on love, art, writing, nature, death, life, and revolution. Digressions come frequently for the spontaneous, discursive style of the *Voyage* resembles that of Laurence Sterne in *Sentimental Journey* and *Tristram Shandy*.

II *References to other Writers*

Cleverly using every trick in the book to hold the reader's attention, Xavier describes the walls in his room. In glancing about, his eyes come to rest on a picture and he speculates about the reader's probable reaction to the scene depicted:

What emotion would he not experience, for example, in contemplating the first print that is presented to his view! He would see there the unhappy *Charlotte*, wiping slowly and with a trembling hand the pistols of *Albert*. Dark presentiment and all the anguish of love without hope and consolation are imprinted on her face, while the cold *Albert*, surrounded by bags of legal documents and old papers of every sort, turns coldly in order to wish a *bon voyage* to his friend. How many times have I not been tempted to break the glass which covers this print, to snatch this *Albert* from his desk, to tear him to pieces, to stamp on him! But there will always be too many

Alberts left in this world. Who is the sensitive man who does not have his, with whom he is obliged to live, and against whom the outpourings of the spirit, the sweet emotions of the heart and the impulses of the imagination proceed to be broken as the waves on the rocks? Happy is he who finds a friend whose heart and mind correspond to his. . . .[81]

Xavier's direct reference to Goethe's *Sufferings of the Young Werther* indicates pre-Romantic learnings. Approval of Werther's suicide is not at issue; rather, the positive qualities inherent in that unfortunate young gentleman are extolled by Xavier. On a personal level he can entertain arguments on the value of subjective reactions to situations in life. Political considerations were another matter. Evidence of sensitivity is not surprising in a writer capable of creating a diverting world of fantasy in the *Voyage*. His acquaintance with *Werther* demonstrates the extent to which he was abreast of the general literary trends in Europe and serves to explain why the *Voyage* proved to be so popular.

To assure the support of readers, Xavier had patterned the *Voyage* somewhat after Sterne's *Sentimental Journey*, a favorite with the French reading public in the eighteenth century along with *Werther*. Since mention of Sterne is then in order, Xavier gladly obliges and, before beginning a discussion on painting, alludes to *Tristram Shandy*: "And this dissertation will be on painting, for there is no way of discoursing on any other subject. I cannot descend completely from the point where I ascended just now; moreover, it is the *hobby* of my Uncle *Toby*."[2]

The purpose of Xavier's reference to Sterne is twofold. He is eager to include Toby in the discussion, and to justify as well the continuation of his room journey. Prior to his remarks on painting and Toby he was excusing himself for giving too free an expression to his emotions and was ready to return to the steadying influence of reason to guide him along a safer course in his armchair travel. This was not to be done, however, at the expense of disrupting altogether the atmosphere of fantasy.

The intensity with which Xavier sympathized with the characters in novels shows his penchant for the imaginative. In Richardson and Goethe Xavier discovers persons with whom he can identify. His susceptibility to emotion-laden passages is easily perceptible and explains why a work like the *Voyage* suited his temperament: "As though I did not have enough troubles, I share willingly those of a thousand imaginary persons, and I feel them as vividly as mine;

how many tears have I not shed for *Clarissa* and for *Charlotte's lover!*"[3]

Like many Frenchmen in the eighteenth century, Xavier was an inveterate reader of sentimental novels and eagerly perused the pages of Prévost. Even though a particular novel by Prévost may exasperate him, once he has begun he cannot put the work aside: "How many times have I not cursed this *Cleveland,* who embarks at every moment on new misfortunes he could avoid. I am unable to bear that book and that chain of calamities; but if I open it absent-mindedly, I must devour it to the very end."[4] Still novels can only partially satisfy Xavier's craving for the type of inspiration that will enable him to explore new worlds, and he soon reaches a saturation point in reading Prévost and Richardson. "When I have had enough of weeping and making love, I seek some poet, and I part anew for another world."[5] Xavier's training in classical languages had a lasting effect on him for the poets to whom he turns are Homer and Virgil. Milton, a modern writer, he judges on the same scale as the great authors of antiquity, also fascinates him. Ossian, as interpreted by Macpherson, may not at first appear to meet the same specifications as the other three poets, but Xavier, like many contemporaries, considered the Gaelic bard a writer of epic proportions. Through the verbal wizardry of these writers he arises to another sphere: "From the expedition of the Argonauts to the assembly of Notables, from the lowest depth of the inferno to the last fixed star beyond the Milky Way, to the limits of the universe, to the gates of chaos, behold the vast field where I proceed to and fro, and at leisure. It is there that I transport my existence, in the wake of *Homer, Milton, Virgil, Ossian,* etc."[6]

Two literary tendencies are discernible in Xavier as he examines the writers he prefers. On one hand the ancients exercise considerable influence on his imagination. "I especially like the poets who transport me into the loftiest antiquity," he admits; "they inspire in me a terror that modern events could not invoke in me."[7] Here a Classical frame of mind manifests itself, for these are the sentiments of the refined aristocrat who countenanced a polished, albeit snobbish, literature fashioned on Greek and Roman models. On the other hand, despite traditional leanings, Xavier unmistakably evinces a taste for the new trend beginning to take shape in French letters. Classical poetry with its pagan mythology strikes a responsive chord in him, as does the mythology of the Bible. Milton, the "sublime blind one of Albion,"[8] captivates Xavier with a superb portrait of Satan, a figure that was to capture the Romantic imagination in France:

> I am unable to keep myself from taking a certain interest in this poor Satan (I speak of *Milton*'s Satan) since he is thus cast from heaven. While condemning the stubbornness of the rebellious mind, I confess that the strength he shows in the excess of misfortune and the grandeur of his courage oblige me to admire him in spite of myself. Although I am not unaware of the misfortunes derived from the deadly undertaking that led him to force the gates of hell to come to disturb our first parents, I cannot, whatever I may do, wish one moment to see him perish en route to the confusion of chaos. . . .[9]

This fascination with Satan is a foretoken of Romanticism, a conclusion warranted by other evidence of Xavier's Romantic instincts—his obsession with sentimental novels, his response to the physical forces and charms of nature, and his overall sensitivity. While an advocate, in general, of the Graeco-Roman literary tradition in the Quarrel of the Ancients and the Moderns, he does not, in the manner of more rabid partisans of the Ancients, object to use of the mythical figures of the Bible as blasphemy. A die-hard Classicist, for that matter, would not respond so enthusiastically to the effusions of Ossian. Another dimension of Xavier's perception of literature and art is revealed in comments on the grandeur of Satan and constitutes a decidedly Gothic element in his aesthetics. Of peripheral interest is a comparison with Joseph's interpretation of Milton's Satan. An admirer of both Shakespeare and Milton, Xavier's older brother did not have the scornful attitude of many French intellectuals toward foreign authors. Joseph, while convinced of the superiority of France's Classical tradition, appreciated Milton's greatness and, although he also had Romantic impulses, was inclined to see in Satan a symbol of a sinister power much like the forces of revolution undermining European society. Both brothers' interpretations of Milton's Satan have a Romantic cast, but Xavier's represents a view that was to be more typical of French Romanticism since he puts aside moral considerations temporarily to study Satan as a fascinating figure, one that excites the imagination.

III   *Attitude toward nature*

Xavier's attitude in the *Voyage* toward nature, the personification of all forces on earth not controlled by man, tends to be Romantic;

like many writers of French Romanticism, he has two different
perceptions of nature. One perspective from which he views nature
suggests the pessimism of Vigny. The death of a friend, now buried
in the cemetery, moves Xavier to realize that his departed comrade
is forgotten by his fellow men. The flora about the grave also show a
similar lack of concern:

> . . . Nature, likewise indifferent to the lot of individuals, puts on its
> brilliant spring robe, and adorns itself in all its beauty around the cemetery
> where he reposes. The trees are covered with leaves and entwine their
> branches; the birds sing under the foliage; the flies buzz among the
> flowers; everything breathes forth joy and life in the sojourn of
> death;—and, in the evening while the moon shines in the sky, and I
> meditate near this sad place, I hear the cricket gaily pursuing his tireless
> song, hidden under the grass, which covers the silent tomb of my
> friend. . . .[10]

Xavier's pessimistic slant on nature does not attain the refined
cynicism of Vigny in which the physical forces about the poet
epitomize the coldness of an unresponsive deity. The author of the
Voyage displays a more conventional reaction typical of Romantics
of the first phase of Romanticism in France (1820 - 1840). His attitude is shaped by Rousseau and the *Night Thoughts* of Young.
Lamartine in the *Méditations* was to strike the same pose in utter-
ing melancholy and subdued reflections on similar subjects. The
sentiments expressed above by Xavier became a Romantic commonplace; man constructs and erects the tombstones and digs the
graves; slowly nature reasserts its dominion, and vines, flowers, and
trees take over the cemetery as manmade objects crumble with
time.

In typical Romantic fashion, Xavier perceives nature differently
in brighter moments and finds there a reflection of man's joys. Then
the young person especially responds to the beauty of the physical
world:

> What a treasure of enjoyment good nature has delivered to men whose
> hearts know how to enjoy! Who can count their innumerable nuances in
> different individuals and in different ages of life? The confused memory of
> those of my childhood still make me tremble. Shall I try to describe that ex-
> perienced by the young man whose heart begins to burn with all the
> passions of sentiment? At this happy age when one is still unaware of the
> name of self-interest, ambition, hatred, and all the shameful passions which

degrade and torment humanity; during this age, alas! too short, the sun shines with a brilliance that is no longer experienced throughout the rest of life. . . .[11]

Xavier was in his thirties when the *Voyage* was completed so some parts probably evince greater maturity. Service against the French and the general disruption brought about by war caused many young men to assume a sober view of society. The overall gaiety that prevails in the *Voyage* recedes in those moments serious questions confront the author. For Xavier his relationship to nature is no laughing matter. Behind the physical forces of the universe he apprehends the God of Christianity. Nature inspires in him alternate moods of sadness and melancholy, of joy and nostalgia, and of earnest meditation on its ultimate significance. Together with Lamartine, he ponders on the marvels of the universe and perceives there a subtle harmony:

The spectacle of nature and contemplating it in its entirety and in detail opens to the mind an immense range of joys. Soon the imagination, soaring over this ocean of pleasure, increases its number and intensity; different sensations are united and combined to form new ones; dreams of glory are intermingled with palpitations of love; benevolence walks next to self-love, which holds out its hand; melancholy comes from time to time to cast over us its solemn mourning crape, and to change our tears into pleasure. . . .[12]

By the 1790s some French writers, thanks to Rousseau and Bernardin de Saint-Pierre, were sensitized to the beauties and the splendor of the physical forces about them. Xavier was one of the best products of this school and, a decade before Chateaubriand, described in exquisite and poetic prose the feelings and sensations evoked in him by nature. His manner of expression is closer to the technique of Rousseau than the methodology employed by Saint-Pierre; the latter made greater use of concrete terms and exotic words in descriptions whereas the former used a minimum of descriptive adjectives and concentrated instead on depicting nature as the vibrant background for the revelation of the artist's thoughts and emotions. Xavier and Lamartine follow much the same pattern. The genius of a Hugo was required to present a detailed and colorful word portrait of nature. Nowhere do Xavier's Romantic tendencies manifest themselves more strongly than in those sections of the *Voyage* where he responds unabashedly to the physical world outside.

IV   *Concept of Time and Dreams*

The reasons for embarking on room travel are not always frivolous, and Xavier, in the early pages of the *Voyage,* hastens to impress this point on readers. One of the oldest dreams of mankind has been to break the barriers imposed on the human spirit by time. An escape from the temporal order is afforded by the imagination, which rises to a level that transcends duration measured by the clock: " . . . Is there a joy more enticing than that of thus extending one's existence, of occupying at the same time the earth and the skies, and of doubling, so to speak, one's being? Is it not the eternal and never satisfied desire of man to increase his potentiality and faculties; to wish to be where he is not, to recall the past and to live in the future? . . ."[13]

Xavier's observation might seem commonplace, but considered in the context of the eighteenth century and with a view to Diderot's speculation on time and the subconscious, his comments acquire deeper meaning. When speaking of an order where past, present, and future tend to merge, Xavier is impinging on an area later to be analyzed more fully by Nodier, Nerval, and Proust. Through the subconscious the creative writer can enter realms not accessible to the average man and expand his faculties to acquire knowledge and insights beyond the scope of pedestrian reason and judgment. When contemplating the possibility of literally doubling his being, Xavier anticipates a literary device in which Nerval was to excel.

Pursuing a pre-Nervalean course, Xavier continues to analyze the promise of a plane of existence in which the clock no longer regulates human activity. There suppressed desires can be realized and the infirmities of age put aside. The parallel with Nerval becomes more striking when Xavier utilizes a portrait in his room as the point of departure for a brief meditation on the meaning of time. It is interesting to note that Xavier's plunge into the depths of the subconscious results from a rather casual act, namely, dusting a picture:

As the cloth took away the dust and brought out blond curls, and the garland of roses with which they are crowned, my soul, from the sun where it had transported itself, felt a light quivering in its heart, and shared sympathetically the enjoyment of my heart. This joy became less confused and more vivid when the cloth, in one single stroke, disclosed the superb forehead of this charming face; my soul was on the verge of leaving the heavens to enjoy this spectacle. . . .[14]

No detailed comparison is necessary to show the extent to which Xavier foreshadowed the technique employed later by Nerval—the portrait as a means to transport readers to the author's plane of timelessness where the past is readily recaptured and associations with comely maidens are frequent. Xavier's intentions are not subject to misinterpretation here, for he states unequivocally his efforts, after admiring the picture, to sever all connections for a moment with the temporal world in order to ascend to a higher and more expansive sphere:

> . . . I existed for an instant in the past, and I rejuvenated against the order of nature. Yes, behold her, this adored woman; it is she; I saw her smiling; she is going to speak in order to say she loves me. What a glance! Come, let me press you to my heart, soul of my life, my second existence! Come share my ecstasy and my happiness! That moment was short but it was ravishing; cold reason soon reasserted its control, and, in the twinkling of an eye, I grew old in a whole year; my heart became cold, frozen, and I found myself on a level with the multitude of indifferent people who are chained to the earth.[15]

Attention should be paid to the clear distinction drawn by Xavier between what amounts to the subconscious or dream state and that of complete consciousness and awareness. Ecstasy and the euphoric sensations of the oneiric world abruptly recede when cold reason resumes its dominion. Similar metaphors are used by Nodier and Nerval when passing from dreams to reality; both writers had Classical and Romantic patches in their makeup. They placed great emphasis on the lucid expression of concepts and, at the same time, delved into the mysteries of the subconscious, one of the lesser known but nonetheless important preoccupations of French Romanticism. It should also be noted that while the *Voyage* is a fantasy, Xavier does not portray dreams and other phenomena of the subconscious as fanciful manifestations of magical powers or as literary motifs adapted from Graeco-Roman models. Instead Xavier treats the subject of dreams and the concept of time as psychological data. An inanimate object, a picture, gives rise to a withdrawal into the past. On another occasion external stimuli might precipitate a series of speculations on the future in light of the knowing subject's past and present experiences. Xavier, like Nerval and Nodier, notifies the reader when a transition is taking place from the wakeful to the oneiric order.

Joseph de Maistre must have discussed the nature of time and the subconscious with his younger brother, since this is one of the central notions advanced in the *Soirées de Saint-Pétersbourg*. When outlining the future role of the poet-prophet, Joseph indicates the unlimited possibilities for artistic creativity in an area where the artist is unhampered by temporalness; there is also in the *Soirées* considerable speculation on the world of the subsconscious as a field as yet unexploited by *littérateurs*. The theosophy of Saint-Martin disclosed to Joseph new concepts of time, impressed upon him the significance of dreams as an important psychic function in man and, in general converted the author of the *Soirées* to irrationalism, the acceptance of unseen forces guiding the universe and intervening in human affairs in a manner beyond the normal powers of deduction. Xavier, while he alludes facetiously to Martinism in the *Voyage*, could not avoid altogether being influenced by Joseph.[16]

Xavier might disclaim any intention of a serious probing into the material and immaterial operations in man, but the evidence in the *Voyage* belies any protestation to the contrary. The author is patently engrossed with data provided by the awareness of his own psyche. It is to his credit that he handles this theme deftly without overburdening the reader with wearisome discourses. Pleasant generalizations about life and the pursuit of happiness have their place in Xavier's view of the universe, but he is sufficiently modern to sense the coming importance of a closer study of the individual. Not overtly subjective, Xavier concentrates on an area that will be of increasing interest to future writers. A prosaic example of the bodily functions of man in contrast to the mental operations is at first sight deceptively simple. Only when applying this distinction to more complicated situations does Xavier reveal the full significance of his treatment of the various stages of man's vegetative, sensory, and intellective functions. The separation of these faculties is most startling to Xavier when he observes his immediate responses to such normal sensations as the body arousing from sound slumber before the soul is fully aware of what is happening:

> . . . *It*[the body] was awake, whether its premature awakening was the effect of nocturnal visions which often put it into a state of agitation as fatiguing as it is useless, or whether the carnival which was coming to an end was the occult cause of its waking up, this time of pleasure and madness having an influence on the human machine as the phases of the moon and the conjunction of certain planets.—In short, it was awake and very much awake, when my soul got rid of the bonds of sleep.[17]

Readers can easily overlook the deeper implications of the foregoing passage, which they accept more often as part and parcel of the
pleasing flights of fancy in the *Voyage*. On closer inspection,
however, there is more than first meets the eye. In *La Fée aux
Miettes*, Nodier uses the same basic data which he enhances to
describe the horrendous sensations experienced by Michel when
awakening from a spine-chilling nightmare; puzzled by these alternate bouts with the conscious and subconscious states, Michel is
forced to conclude that perhaps the dream world represents after all
the ultimate reality. Xavier is not concerned with developing his
findings in such detail. As a product of the eighteenth century he
merely comments rather factually about his observations on the
conscious and subconscious in man.

Xavier never ceases to intrigue today's readers of the *Voyage* with
his ability to intuit future trends in the literary treatment of dreams
and the subconscious. One such example is the description of Xavier
dozing off peacefully and then being aroused abruptly by the valet,
Joannetti:

I snoozed imperceptibly while the water was warming. I was enjoying
this pleasure which I have told my readers about, and that one experiences
when one feels one's self going asleep. The soothing sound Joannetti was
making in bumping the coffee pot on the andiron resounded in my brain,
and caused all my sensitive fibers to vibrate, as the plucking of a harp cord
makes the octaves resound. Finally I saw something like a shadow before
me; I opened my eyes; it was Joannetti. Ah! What an aroma! What a pleasant surprise! Coffee! Cream! A pile of toast! Good reader, dine with me.[18]

At first glance there would not be a ready association with an
eerie passage from Nerval's haunting tale, *Soirée d'automne*, yet
there are striking points of similarity. In both the *Voyage* and *Soirée
d'automne* a servant awakens the author from a dream or reverie in
the course of which there is a confusion of sensations and the impression of indefiniteness as though reality and unreality are not
clearly delineated. What is nothing more than a comfortable and
drowsy reaction on Xavier's part is for Nerval a traumatic moment
as the valet arouses him from an ominous nightmare. In the latter
case Nerval's experience amounts to a terrifying hallucination in
which sensory impressions haunt and trouble the writer's memory
long after awakening. Once again the difference between the
handling of dreams in writings of the Enlightenment and Romanticism is brought into sharp contrast. Unlike Nerval, Xavier has the

carefree approach of the empiricist who calmly notes his own reactions. The reference to "sensitive fibers" is reminiscent of similar jargon employed by Diderot in explaining the physiology of the body's reaction to external stimuli. Although Nerval in *Soirée d'automne* was directly inspired by Hoffmann, the facts indicate that Xavier was moving a step further than Diderot and the *philosophes* in the continuing exploration of the subconscious. Mention by Xavier of coffee and toast brings to mind the crumbs in the teacup immortalized by Proust in *La Recherche du temps perdu.*

The brief incursions into the subconscious have not been without their rewards. As a result of his investigation, Xavier emerges with keener insights into his own psyche. The return to consciousness is in a measure welcome, for he takes with him the memory of an unusual and fruitful experience: "However, never have I perceived more clearly that I am *double*. While I miss my fanciful pleasures, I feel perforce consoled; a secret power carries me along;—it tells me I need the fresh air and solitude resembles death. . . ."[19]

While Xavier freely engages in what might be termed literary dreams, a convenient device for creative writing, these dreams still conform in a measure to present-day medical definitions. Dreaming, according to many psychologists, represents a wish to realize in sleep desires unattainable in waking life. Pleasant dreams allow the individual to remain sleeping and, conversely, unpleasant dreams cause so much anxiety that the individual wakes up. The sensation of great anxiety on awakening is called a nightmare. Xavier also concerns himself with fantasy, a deliberate process whereby an individual makes up a story or situation to fulfill a need or wish that cannot be satisfied in reality.

In the case of Nodier and Nerval, their obsession with oneiric data justifies the assumption that the dreams and nightmares described in their writings are connected in some manner with their personal lives. There is patently more to the dreams depicted by Nodier and Nerval than the manifest content or material from ordinary events in one's life that enter into the fashioning of the dream; what also must be taken into consideration is the latent content—the free associations, experiences, or conflicts that comprise the underlying cause of the dream. Xavier's dreams do not fit into these categories. Besides, he indulges as well in daydreams; the latter are imaginary events in which the subject participates more or less voluntarily. Where Xavier records dreams directly traceable to recent events, the content is reportable and analyzable, for he is concerned especially with the physiological features of dreaming. Nodier and Nerval, on the other hand, present a more complex problem to the student since their latent dream material ostensibly stems from both past and recent experiences, often traumatic in nature, while with Xavier oneiric themes are primarily a literary motif.

V   *Xavier's Use of Fantasy*

With a view to holding the reader's interest, Xavier explains the process by which persons slip into the realm of fantasy. It can happen unexpectedly: "When you read a book, sir, and a more agreeable idea suddenly enters your imagination, your soul is immediately attached to it and forgets the book, while your eyes follow mechanically the words and the lines; you finish the page without understanding it and without remembering what you read. . . ."[20]

Xavier soon discovers an overlapping of the fantasy and the dream. The more he gives rein to his imagination in conjuring up pleasant thoughts and images the more he withdraws from the world of consciousness. Slowly, almost imperceptibly, he lapses into a dream state literally hypnotized by the object of his contemplation, but still has total recall of the process that took place in the transition from fantasizing to dreaming: "Be that as it may, While I was abandoning myself to these reflections, my eyes finally closed, and I fell sound asleep; but, on closing my eyes, the image of the persons about whom I had thought remained painted on that fine canvas called *memory*. . . ."[21]

By dealing with fantasy as a vehicle for literary expression, Xavier was perpetuating a trend already well established in French letters since the Middle Ages. Moliere's comedies abound in marvelous moments of verbal fantasy and even Corneille's *L'Illusion comique* offered some striking examples of an adroit application of this particular technique. While Pierre-Georges Castex in *Le Conte fantastique en France* does not include Xavier among writers of this genre, the *Voyage* does nonetheless comform in part to some of the criteria for a tale of the preternatural or irrational. Heine always denied that a *Conte fantastique* could be written by a Frenchman, and maintained that this genre, essentially Germanic, was foreign to the Gallic spirit.[22] Xavier, however, belies the judgment of the German poet. Although the *Voyage* by no stretch of the imagination

even begins to penetrate the world of the preternatural, there are
still many elements in Xavier's work found in the *Conte fantastique*—the use of mirrors and pictures to conjure up images in
the reader's mind, the constant flitting back and forth in time, and
the soul-beast relationship; the latter element would lend itself well
to a Gothic treatment. There is no denying that Xavier's sprightly
little treatise ran the gamut of literary devices and motifs.

VI   *The Soul-Beast Relationship*

One of the first points students learned in years past, when the
Voyage autour de ma chambre was studied in school, was Xavier's
description of the soul-beast relationship. It was his entertaining
way of differentiating between mind and body functions. In
Chapter VI of the *Voyage* he lays down the guidelines for his distinction between *l'âme* and *la bête*, a distinction he uses to good
effect throughout the room journey to titillate the reader:

> This chapter is absolutely only for metaphysicians. It is going to throw
> the greatest light on the nature of man; it is the prism with which one can
> analyze and break down the faculties of man, by separating the animal
> power from the pure rays of reason.
> It would be impossible for me to explain how and why I burnt my fingers
> in the first steps I took on beginning my trip, without explaining in the
> greatest detail to the reader my system of *the soul and the beast*. This
> metaphysical discovery above all has such an influence on my ideas and ac-
> tions, that it would be very difficult to understand this book if I did not give
> the key at the beginning.
> I noticed through various observations that man is composed of a soul
> and a beast. These two beings are absolutely distinct, but so interlocked one
> in the other, or one on the other that the soul has to have a certain
> superiority over the beast to be in a position to make the distinction.[23]

As casual as Xavier's approach is to an exceedingly complicated
topic, it is clear he speaks from a certain philosophical frame of
reference and one that is not Cartesian. Soul and body form a
oneness, and both are necessary to complete this unit; neither one
can function without the other. The Cartesian division between
mind and matter is absent. A product of Catholic training, Xavier
adopts here a distinction patently borrowed from Aristotle and
Thomas Aquinas. Soul and body are sharply differentiated and,
contrary to eighteenth century rationalism, Xavier speaks in terms
of material and spiritual faculties in man. However, he does allude

to specific physiological and psychological functions in a manner that indicates an acquaintance with the *philosophes*. Xavier injects a gay note into what might otherwise be a ponderous discussion on metaphysics by a reference to burnt fingers, empirical evidence of a sensory reaction of which the mind takes note. In a further effort to avoid a heavy-footed narrative, he jauntily labels the beast *l'autre*—the other.

The mind-body distinction in the Enlightenment was not a problem considered just by the *philosophes*. A concurrent movement, theosophy, also dwelt upon the same question. Chief among the theosophists, men who claimed to have direct access to some form of supernatural revelation, was Swedenborg. The Scandinavian mystic often spoke of his spirit's departure from the body to travel at will in the heaven and the planets. Xavier at one point gives what appears to be a Swedenborgian description of the spirit leaving the body when he outlines the advantages of "having a soul detached from matter to the point of having it travel all alone when deemed fitting."[24]

From the standpoint of modern psychiatry, Xavier's separation of the two faculties is reasonably accurate. Many present-day psychiatrists divide brain functions into lower and higher levels. The lower or sensory level includes conscious awareness, and reaction to the body and its instincts and to stimuli of the outside world. On this lower level are the id, or instincts, as well as certain parts of the ego, or awareness. At the higher level, judgmental and intellective operations are carried out in the area of thinking, remembering, comparing, problem-solving, verbalizing, and consulting past experience. Although Xavier is far from probing so deeply into the human psyche, he does recognize a few basic psychiatric principles. The extent of his investigations is revealed in his treatment of the subconscious in the *Voyage*.

One critic in particular, Jules Clarétie, went overboard in extolling the originality of Xavier's dichotomy and made sweeping statements, some of which were slightly unwarranted:

What certainly belongs to Xavier de Maistre is indeed originality, and perhaps also the *boldness* of his book, this now immortal philosophical theory of the *beast* and the *soul*. . . . There is *an entire system* in the little metaphysical discovery which he seems to want to make fun of. . . . One would have without doubt astonished the author of the *Voyage autour de ma chambre* very much, if one had told him his system could, strictly speaking, support those *materialists*, anathematized by Joseph de Maistre, and who claim that the body has a decisive influence over the mind. . . .[25]

Clarétie is correct in noting the originality of Xavier's charming presentation of an important principle of psychology, but he goes too far in labeling Xavier a materialist. The Thomism to which he was exposed in Chambéry admitted the same distinctions, a fact of which Berthier is cognizant when he makes pertinent and perceptive comments in refuting Clarétie:

> Certainly, if the system in question contained a grain of *materialism*, the philosophical ideas that we are going to expound would be the formal condemnation of them. Let us observe that in the thinking of Xavier, *the beast* is not precisely *the body*, but rather the sensitive principle that the Latins called *anima*—and that by soul he understands *animus*, the knowing mind. . . .[26]

Thus, Berthier's remarks substantiate the position taken in this chapter, namely, that the soul-beast relationship described by Xavier embraces many specific and complex functions of the higher and lower levels of the psyche.

Although caution should generally be exercised in any attempt to discern Freudian themes, particularly in a writer of a period long before the birth of the Viennese psychiatrist, the soul-beast relationship does offer a few provocative parallels with some of the cardinal principles in Freud's thinking. To simplify somewhat an extremely complex system, the *id* can be considered as the collection of instinctual drives seeking to assert themselves; the *ego* coordinates the personality; and the *superego* assumes some of the functions traditionally ascribed to conscience. These three operations of the psyche, as outlined by Freud, are approximated by Xavier in one of the descriptions of the soul-beast relationship. On this particular occasion there is a confrontation as a result of the soul's dream about Mme Hautcastel. The beast is furious when the soul accuses it of not behaving properly when a dream is in progress. Since the beast is on the instinctive level, and the soul, in this case, make judgments and plays the role of conscience, they resemble respectively the *id* and the *superego*. Xavier passively comments on the argument between the beast and the soul and sounds, for a moment, like the *ego* coordinating the two other disparate functions of the psyche. The immediate cause of the altercation is the beast's alleged misconduct while the soul was in dreamland paying a visit to Mme Hautcastel. Enraged, the latter upbraids the beast in no uncertain terms. Xavier all the while casually relates the bitter exchange: "What! said my soul, is it thus that, during my absence, instead of resting your strength by a peaceful sleep, and making yourself better prepared thereby to carry out my orders, you *insolently* (the term was a little strong) decide to indulge in imaginings that my will has not sanctioned?"[27]

The issue is complicated at this point by Xavier's allusion to a Thomistic concept in which the beast is given a role more important than the primitive level represented by the function of the external senses alone. In Thomistic psychology, one of the main internal senses is the imagination, a faculty capable of producing a concrete image of one single fact of sensory experience as opposed to the intellect's ability to form universal ideas derived from a wide range of sensory data. The beast indulges in imaginings and incurs the wrath of the soul acting for all the world like Freud's *superego*. Not to be outdone the beast, or *id*, instinctively accuses the soul of not always conforming to the canons of propriety:

> . . . It certainly suits you to take on airs of decency and virtue! Do I not owe everything you do not like to . . . your imagination and extravagant ideas? Why were you not there? Why should you have the right to enjoy the frequent trips you take alone without me? Have I ever disapproved your seances in the empyrean or in the Elysian fields, your conversations with intellects, your profound speculations (a little irony, as one sees), your castles in Spain, your sublime systems? And should I not have the right, when you abandon me thus, to enjoy the benefits and the pleasures accorded and presented to me by nature![28]

What takes place in the squabble between the beast and the soul is after a fashion an inner conflict. There is an overlapping of functions, as it is the *ego*, rather than the *superego*, that usually enters into conflict with the *id*. Be that as it may, Xavier resolves the dispute by having Joannetti prepare coffee. There remains, nonetheless, significant evidence of the author's probing into psychological phenomena later explored in greater depth in the nineteenth century by psychiatrists and writers. (No conclusions need be drawn here on the sexual life of Xavier, who is primarily concerned with sustaining the reader's interest in the room journey by entertaining digressions.) Unquestionably the author has a continued preoccupation with dreams and the subconscious throughout the *Voyage*. This preoccupation may be expressed in pre-Freudian terms, in a Neoplatonic description of "conversations with intellects," and in Thomistic views on psychology, but the evidence is undeniably there. A question might well be raised, it would seem, on the extent of Xavier's influence in this regard on French Romanticism, especially in light of the widespread popularity of the *Voyage autour de ma chambre* in the pre-Romantic era. Without doubt there is more contained in Xavier's soul-beast distinction than first meets the eye.

VII   *Feminine Ideal*

A significant and delightful motif in the *Voyage* is Xavier's vision of the feminine ideal that assumes several forms, the most frequent being that of Mme Hautcastel, in all probability a lady he met in the salons of Turin. Her picture is a point of departure for Xavier's discourses on love and beauty. A withered rose reminds him of one particular encounter with Mme Hautcastel. The lovely lady, unmoved by Xavier's tender display of esteem as he offered her the flower, is more concerned about her gown:

. . . She took it and put it on her dressing-table without looking at it and without looking at me. But how would she have paid attention to me! She was busy looking at herself. Standing before a large mirror with her hair set, she was putting the finishing touches to her adornment; she was so preoccupied, her attention was so totally absorbed by ribbons, muslin, and tassels of all kinds piled up before her, that I did not receive even a glance, a sign. . . .[29]

The propensity on Xavier's part to delight in recalling such moments cannot help but remind readers of Nerval's obsession with reliving moments in an idealized past when in fantasy events were fashioned to correspond to a reality Gérard wanted but never knew. Rousseau, in the *Confessions*, utilized a similar technique, and while he undoubtedly altered the facts somewhat, he did not retreat totally into a world of unreality. Xavier represents in a sense a transitional stage between Rousseau and Nerval in the evolution of the flashback about fair ladies. The author of the *Voyage* goes a step further than Rousseau by associating his remembrance of former incidents to some extent with the workings of the subconscious. Nerval picks up where Xavier leaves off and develops in much greater detail the process of a vivid recall of an idealized past with a clear reference to present happenings and a lucid description of the stages through which the mind passes from wakefulness to the nebulous zone of the subconscious.

Unmistakably Xavier in the course of his room journey and imaginary visits to fair ladies examines the steps whereby the mind drifts almost imperceptibly from the waking state to semi-consciousness, and then into slumber. In relating one of his encounters with Mme Hautcastel, Xavier has difficulty in recalling just what transpired as he began to fall asleep and dream of the pretty and imperious lady. Objects in Xavier's room associated with Mme Hautcastel—flowers, veiling, and a lock of hair—help to lend an air of reality to the dream:

. . . I had progressed completely to a state hard to describe, when finally my soul, either through sagacity or through chance, found the way of delivering itself from the veiling suffocating it. I do not know whether it discovered an opening, or whether it simply decided to lift it up, which is more natural; the fact is it found the way out of the labyrinth. The lock of hair in disarray was still there; but it was no longer an obstacle, it was rather a means; my soul seized it as a man who is drowning hangs on to the grass on the bank; but the string of pearls broke in the struggle, and the scattering beads rolled on the sofa and from there onto the floor of Mme de Hautcastel; for, my mind, through a bizarre act that it would be difficult to explain rationally, imagined itself at the home of this lady; a big bouquet of violets fell on the floor, and my soul, awakening then, returned to its abode, bringing in its wake reason and reality. . . .[30]

What is quickly noted in Xavier's description is his ability to select specific physical objects that convey to the reader some sense of the sensations experienced in a dream; locks of hair and, especially, veiling have physical properties that in a skillful word portrait assume an oneiric quality. Water in particular has a fluidity, reproducing in descriptions of dreams the amorphousness connected with the ever-changing states of the subconscious. Hence Xavier's symbol of the swimmer floundering in the water represents a rather advanced technique in the use of the oneiric theme in literature. Even more sophisticated is the utilization of the feminine ideal with a chameleonic presence and one whose mood is totally unpredictable.

VIII   *French Revolution*

One of the grimmest subjects considered in the *Voyage* is the sanguinary events of the French Revolution. Xavier's emotional response is understandable in light of the invasion of Sardinia by the ragged, fanatical soldiers of the First Republic. The loyal monarchist did not welcome them as liberators, but judged them to be the legions of anarchy in its worst form. Its effect on Xavier is forcefully demonstrated when the author likens the outbreak of a rebellion to the unexpected appearance of a savage beast on the stage before an elegant crowd of theatergoers while a performance is in progress:

> . . . When I am at one of these entertainments, in the midst of this crowd of pleasant men who dance, sing, cry at tragedies, express only joy, frankness, and cordiality, I say to myself: "Suppose there suddenly entered this polite assembly a white bear, a philosopher, or some other animal of this species, who, climbing into the orchestra, shouted in a wild voice: 'Wretched humans! Listen to the truth spoken to you through my mouth; you are oppressed, tyrannized; you are unhappy, you are bored. Abandon this lethargy!
>
> 'You, musicians, start by breaking these instruments over your heads; let everyone arm himself with a dagger; henceforth think no longer about relaxation and entertainment; climb into the boxes, wipe out everybody; let the ladies dip their timid hands in blood too!
>
> 'Leave, you are *free;* snatch your king from his throne, and your God from his sanctuary!' "[31]

Xavier is so terrified by the prospect of a similar blood bath in Sardinia that he orders the valet to bolt the doors and seizes his sword. The threat to throne and altar, two institutions dear to his heart, is more than he can bear. From the trauma experienced by Xavier it is not difficult to deduce one of the motives in writing the *Voyage*—a means of escaping temporarily the hardships brought about by the French Revolution. As with Joseph de Maistre, the civil upheaval in France left its scars on Xavier's memory, and he speculates on the probable reaction of a famous Greek leader to the horrors of the violence in Paris:

> *Pericles,* who had approached the window, took a deep sigh; I guessed the reason for it. He was reading an issue of the *Moniteur* that announced the decline of the arts and sciences; he saw illustrious men leaving their sublime speculations to invent new crimes; and he trembled to hear a horde

of cannibals comparing themselves to the heroes of generous Greece, doom-
ing to the scaffold, without shame and remorse, venerable old men,
women, children; committing coldbloodedly the most atrocious and useless
crimes.[32a]

Without the means of directly identifying the preceding quota-
tion, readers could justifiably attribute it to Joseph de Maistre, for
in tone and irony the passage has the flavor of the older brother's
diatribes against unrestrained republicanism and the demagogues
who lead the masses astray. Xavier may have been somewhat less
dogmatic than Joseph on a few issues in the 1790s, but he definitely
joined the latter in condemning what they both considered the
satanic forces of anarchy.

IX   *Relevance to Contemporary Problems*

"And why would I involve myself in considering those who are in
a more agreeable situation, while the world swarms with people
more unfortunate than I am in mine?"[32] Xavier pauses in the
Voyage to ponder on the inequities in the social order he knew. His
question could be repeated with even greater meaning today, when
modern communications have increased the awareness of existing
injustice on a global scale. He fights off a feeling of guilt about an
overriding involvement in his fantasies to observe for a moment the
society about him:

Instead of transporting myself through the imagination into this superb
abode where so many beauties are eclipsed by the young *Eugénie,* to be
happy I have only to stop an instant along the streets that lead there. A pile
of wretches, sleeping half-naked under the portals of these sumptuous
apartments, seem on the verge of expiring from cold and misery. What a
sight! I would like this page of my book known by all the world; I would
like people to know that, in this city, where everything exudes opulence,
during the coldest nights in winter, a crowd of wretches sleeps without
shelter, with their heads resting on a boundary marker or on the threshold
of a palace:
Here, it is a group of children hugging one another in order not to die of
cold. There, it is a woman shivering without a voice to complain. The
passers-by come and go, without being disturbed by a sight to which they
are accustomed: The noise of the carriages, the voice of intemperance, the
delightful sounds of music, intermingle sometimes with the screams of
these wretches, and form a horrible dissonance.[33]

Xavier's sensitivity to social injustice expressed here is indeed significant. Not every writer of the early nineteenth century reacted so compassionately to privation and suffering, particularly one who was himself an aristocrat and a career officer in the army of an absolute monarch. The urban theme enters the narrative at this point, disclosing the multifaceted viewpoint of Xavier in the *Voyage*. In what was originally intended to be a lighthearted fantasy, the author suddenly takes a serious turn in the course of his room journey and examines the social scene about him. Such insights would never occur to him unless he had previous contact with the unfortunate members of society, a process that would acquaint him with the victims of human indifference. It is not necessary to look very far for the root causes of Xavier's commiseration with the downtrodden. The *philosophes* commented on the lot of the poor; still theirs was an elitist perspective, and they often tended to theorize instead of offering a practical program to remedy wrongs in the social order. In addition to the *philosophes*, Xavier could also draw on his experience in Chambéry. Together with Joseph he was associated with groups of laymen who cared for the needs of prisoners rotting away in foul dungeons.

Xavier, after having depicted the callous attitude of many citizens toward their fellowmen, hastens to present the other side of the picture. Not everyone is oblivious to misery. Very often humanitarians quietly go about their good deeds:

> . . . I have spoken of the poor people that are found there, of their pitiful cries, and of the indifference of certain persons in their regard; but I have said nothing of the great number of charitable men who sleep while the others are having a good time, who arise at daybreak and go to help the suffering without being seen and without ostentation.[34]

The author balances the often carefree tone of the *Voyage* with a timely lesson in Christian charity. As already stated, he was indebted to the *philosophes* and the example of dedicated coreligionists in Chambéry for the ability to empathize immediately with the less fortunate. The thought of zealous individuals, practicing their principles without fanfare, apparently inspired in Xavier a fit setting for a painting as he imagined them going to church after having first carried out the teachings of the social gospel. A Chateaubriandesque cast is perceptible in the following scene depicted by Xavier:

After having thus shared their fortune with their brethren, after having poured balm into these hearts torn with pain, they go into the churches, while weary vice sleeps on the eiderdown quilt, to offer their prayers to God and to thank him for his largess: the light of the solitary lamp in the temple still resists the light of the new day, and already they are prostrate at the foot of the altars;—and the Eternal, irritated by the hardness and avarice of men, holds back his lightning ready to strike![35]

The eucharistic presence patently furnished Xavier with considerable inspiration in this word portrait. Little analysis is required to associate the idealistic picture painted by Xavier with some of the central ideas in Chateaubriand. The soft light in the shadows of the church in early morn invites the worshiper to adore the Lord in the tabernacle; that divine presence is symbolized by the vigil light in the sanctuary. Lamartine developed the same theme in poems of the *Harmonies* and *Méditations*. Clearly Xavier was thinking in definitely Romantic terms when he treated the seamy side of life in the *Voyage*. His response was like that of many writers in the initial phase of French Romanticism—a sensitivity to the aesthetic features of Catholic liturgy and sympathy with the disadvantaged. Perhaps the most modern aspect of Xavier's perception of the social problems of his time is a form of big city neurosis that overwhelms him. Indifference to inequities and injustice by implication is found more often in a metropolis. While present-day urban sprawl was unknown to Xavier, he nonetheless perceives the unhappy consequences of overpopulation.

Another consequence of a complicated pattern of living is war. Xavier's recollections of recent battles between the Sardinians and the French lead him to recall a pleasant association with a comrade-in-arms: ". . . We sustained one another in the painful tasks of war; we had only one pipe for the two of us; we drank from the same cup; we slept under the same canvas, and, in the unhappy circumstances in which we were, the place where we lived together was a new country: I have seen him subject to all the perils of war, and of a disastrous war. . . ."[36]

Ironically, Xavier's friend died of sickness and not in battle. This sad end of a brave soldier troubles Xavier, for it reveals to him the emptiness of existence and, unknowingly, he has a feeling of alienation, a decidedly twentieth century emotion. Probably when he first conceived the format of the *Voyage* Xavier did not forsee the results of his speculations on a variety of subjects. In seeking to add variety to an account of armchair travel, Xavier delves into grave and far-reaching problems, political and social:

> . . . Death seemed to spare us for each other; she exhausted her strikes a thousand times around him without reaching him; but it was in order to make his loss more painful to me. The tumult of arms, the enthusiasm that takes hold of the soul at the prospect of danger, would have perhaps kept his cries from going right to my heart. His death would have been useful to his country and terrible to the enemy:—I would have missed him less. But to lose him in the middle of the enjoyments of a winter period! to see him die in my arms at the moment when he seemed to be bursting with health.[37]

What conclusion does Xavier draw from this bleak picture? "The insensitive destruction of beings and all the misfortunes of humanity are counted for nothing in the overall scheme of things."[38] This bitter reflection brings to mind similar ones by Camus and Saint-Exupéry when relating their impressions of the lot of individuals in a universe governed by unseen and inexorable forces. In such a world, they conclude with Xavier, only personal friendships and values have any meaning.

Among other themes in the *Voyage* that have been enlarged upon by writers in the nineteenth and twentieth centuries is that of the individual in a mass society. Xavier touches on this dilemma in one of the descriptions of the beast functioning alone unaided by the soul. Surrounded by a throng of people, the individual very often still has a haunting sense of loneliness:

> . . . Look at the beast, cast into the world having run all alone the course of fortune and honors; see with what gravity it walks among men; the crowd steps aside with respect, and, believe me, no one will notice that it is all alone; it is the least concern of the throng in whose midst it is walking, to know whether it has a soul or not, whether it thinks or not. . . .[39]

The foregoing theme of course was dear to the heart of Baudelaire, disgusted with the callousness of the bourgeois milieu in which he languished. Although sharply different in motivation, Xavier shared some mutual insights with Baudelaire. Solitude in a crowd is a distinctly Baudelairean motif, and Xavier displayed a clairvoyance beyond the ken of most of his contemporaries in sensing the inability of the creative spirit to adapt completely to a crass, industrial existence. Along with Baudelaire, Xavier appreciated the value of individuality, and in a reflection in a mirror beheld a picture of indisputable uniqueness:

Well! what a picture could be presented to you gentlemen; what a sight could be set before your eyes, ladies, more certain of your approval than the faithful representation of yourselves? The picture of which I speak is a mirror, and no one up to the present has yet decided to criticize it; it is, for all those who look at it, a perfect picture, about which there is nothing more to say.[40]

Solitude, even in a crowd, and the significance of one's reflection in a mirror were motifs utilized in the *Petits poémes en prose* to emphasize Baudelaire's message of the pricelessness of individuality in a society cheapened by bourgeois values.

X *Painting versus Music*

Throughout the *Voyage* Xavier demonstrates that the word portrait is his forte through his capacity for depicting the objects in his room succinctly and graphically. His talents in this regard are not limited to the material order, for he creates lucid verbal impressions of the highly intangible realm of the dream and the subconscious. There is no mistaking the fact that Xavier is an intensely visual writer. Sound is one sensory stimulus that has minimal appeal to him. Memories of the past will conjure up sights not sounds, a reaction not surprising in a painter. From all reports, Xavier's landscapes and portraits were conventional and showed considerable skill if not the genius necessary for a great artist. None of his paintings are on display today in museums and many have been destroyed. The few that remain belong to descendants of the Maistre family.

Xavier's preoccupation with the visual arts produced some surprising statements in the *Voyage* where his hostility to sound as an artistic medium is expressed with astonishing vehemence: "Music is subject to fashion, and art is not." The former is disgustingly ephemeral in character: "Musical pieces that delighted our predecessors are ridiculous to the art lovers of our day." Painting on the other hand, has an enduring quality: "Raphael's paintings will charm our children as they enthralled our ancestors."[41] Not content with relegating music to an insignificant category Xavier contemptuously dismisses it as a base skill making no demands on the intellective and creative faculties: ". . . You see children playing the piano like great masters; you have never seen a good painter twelve years old. Painting, besides taste and feeling, requires a thinking head, which musicians can do without. You see everyday brainless and heartless men drawing charming sounds from a violin, from a harp."[42]

Did *Bans* fail to learn how to play an instrument to the ridicule of his peers? Was he sick and tired of the endless squabble over the relative merits of Italian as opposed to French music? The facts may never be known, but readers can probably be thankful for his prejudice. Without it he might not have excelled to the extent he did in the word portrait, a talent that stood him in good stead when depicting the picturesque ambiance of the *Prisonniers du Caucase* and *La Jeune Sibérienne*.

XI *Conclusion*

The *Voyage autour de ma chambre* upon analysis is a fruitful work indeed for students of literary history. In its pages can be detected the germs of many ideas and themes to be utilized by Romantic writers. Investigations of the subconscious and the psyche touched on areas fraught with implications. From the standpoint of sociology he noted briefly but astutely the presence of urban problems, alienation, and overpopulation. As a soldier, the evils of war were of course all too apparent to him. On this subject and on the topic of the French Revolution he shared some of the apocalyptic vision of Joseph. Subsequent writers were to explore in greater depth other themes treated in the *Voyage*. Baudelaire summed up the motif of big city loneliness and the loss of individuality in a metropolitan setting. Lamartine, drawing as Xavier did on Ossian and Young, enlarged upon the melancholy and meditative aspects of nature. Nodier devoted more attention to the hallucinatory features of dreams and nightmares, while Nerval would pursue in his haunting writings the fleeting vision of the feminine ideal. Those readers of the nineteenth century who dismissed the *Voyage* as a quaint but inconsequential book failed to peruse its contents thoughtfully and observantly.

CHAPTER 3

Expédition nocturne autour de ma chambre

I *Introduction*

THE *Expédition nocturne autour de ma chambre* was published in 1825 at Paris by Dondey-Dupré. The period of
composition was from 1799 to 1823, twenty-four years in all, and
covered the time of Xavier's sojourn in Russia, his service in the
czar's army, and the first years of his marriage. The attic flat
described by Xavier was one he actually occupied on a side street in
Turin and, as in the *Voyage*, there are allusions to actual persons
and events.

II *Analysis of Narrative*

Upon learning that Buffon took refuge from worldly cares in a
sequestered house on a quiet lane, Xavier decides to profit by that
philosopher's example and remove himself from the whirl of social
activities by seeking solitude in an out-of-the-way apartment on a
side street, far from the main thoroughfare. There are as usual
obstacles to the preparations for another room journey. Xavier's new
domestic lacks the finesse of Joannetti and is extremely bothersome.
Once located in his new surroundings, however, Xavier is easily
lulled into a meditative revery:

. . . I had transported there on the same day the materials for my
favorite occupations, and I spent most of my time in the process, sheltered
from disturbance by servants and the cleaners of the paintings. The hours
flowed by for me like minutes in this isolated spot, and more than once my
reveries made me forget the dinner hour.
O sweet solitude! I am acquainted with the charms with which you in-
toxicate lovers. Misfortune be upon the one who cannot be one day alone in

his life without experiencing the torment of boredom, and who prefers, if
need be, to converse with fools rather than with himself.[1]

Settled down once more with the furniture and belongings that
provided the background for the previous trip, Xavier regrets the
absence of the faithful Joannetti. The replacement is a rogue whose
surreptitious activity injects a comical note into the narrative.
Though annoyed at apprehending the rascal in the act of stealing
some of his effects, Xavier is amused by the culprit's reaction:

> . . . If someone wanted to paint the expression of amazement and fright
> registered to the highest degree on the human face, he would have been
> the perfect model when he saw me at his side. I had all the leisure time to
> study it; for he was so disconcerted by my unexpected appearance and the
> seriousness with which I looked at him that he continued to walk for a while
> with me without saying a word, as if we had been on the walk to-
> gether. . . .[2]

With unconcealed pleasure Xavier summarily discharges the un-
trustworthy fellow, but the feeling of relief is short-lived. With the
sensitivity so characteristic of his narrative style, Xavier voices simply and unaffectedly the deep sorrow caused by the absence of the
two companions on his previous trip, Rosine and Joannetti. Further
grief is occasioned by memories of the site of the first room journey
long since destroyed in the war. Xavier delicately recreates the illusion of countries visited and sustains the element of fantasy
necessary in such writings. Readers are reassured that he will make
an effort to recapture the delights of the initial venture in armchair
travel:

> I had been wishing for a long time to see again the country I had former-
> ly passed through so pleasantly, and whose description did not seem com-
> plete to me. Some friends who had enjoyed it entreated me to continue it,
> and I would have made up my mind sooner without doubt, if I had not
> been separated from my travel companions. I was resuming my course
> regretfully. Alas! I was returning there alone. . . .[3]

The departure of a servant and the aging of a pet may seem of little consequence but in Xavier's eyes these events become symbols
of the relentless passing of time and the lack of permanence in
human relations. The blending of humor and pathos in the *Expédi-*

tion nocturne escapes the pitfalls of banality thanks to Xavier's straightforwardness and unpretentiousness. When the old and doddering Rosine tries to follow Joannetti about, to leave Xavier to get married, the valet brings him back to his master. The author sees in this an unhappy reflection of the ephemeralness of the human condition:

> . . . I saw Joannetti's hand push her into the room; the door was shut again and I felt my heart tighten. Already he is no longer entering my room. A few minutes have sufficed to make two old companions for fifteen years strangers to each other. O sad, sad plight of humanity, never being able to find a single, stable object in which to place the least of one's affections![4]

Besides Rosine and Joannetti, Xavier loses another presence on this second trip when he decides to eliminate any reference to the soul and the beast. The author, in so doing, gives the impression that in some respects at least he intends to make the voyage less fanciful and speculative this time. Perhaps the stress of the French Revolution and the Napoleonic wars caused him to counter-balance realistic and imaginative elements even in a fantasy. A letter from a girlfriend, ending their association, strengthens his resolution to discard themes that smack of idealism and for a moment he resolves to be more pragmatic:

> . . . Since that fatal day I decided to advance my system of the soul and the beast no longer. Consequently, without making any distinction between these two beings and without separating them, I will have them pass along carrying each other, as certain merchants do their merchandise, and I will travel as a unit in order to avoid any inconvenience.[5]

There are, nonetheless, attractive features to the second trip. The contemplation of the beauties of nature, one of the high points of the first journey, is a luxury in which Xavier indulges at his leisure. Owing to the peculiar construction of his attic flat, he must ascend several rungs of a small ladder to peek out of the window. The panorama below does not constantly meet his eyes and become a boring commonplace. Instead, it requires some effort on his part to enjoy the awe-inspiring spectacle outside. Xavier explains how a seemingly inconsequential part of a daily routine becomes an esthetic experience:

. . . But the most beautiful view soon tires us when seen too often. The eyes get used to it and you no longer pay any attention. The location of my window preserved me again from this disadvantage, because I never saw the magnificent sight of the countryside of Turin without climbing four or five steps, which always procured for me vivid enjoyment, because it was controlled. When, fatigued, I wished to provide myself an agreeable recreation, I ended my day by climbing up to my window.[6]

As to be expected, much of the pleasure Xavier derives from this new room journey is obtained from the freedom he enjoys to meditate and daydream whenever he wishes. Anxious to give readers the sense of actual participation and not merely a vague, vicarious experience, Xavier urges them to take an active role and to explore the realm of fantasy for themselves. This invitation is issued to those with a lively imagination who are dissatisfied with a humdrum existence:

. . . A troublesome feeling, however, disturbed the pleasure I experienced in entering into these meditations. How few persons, I said to myself, now enjoy with me the sublime spectacle that the heaven displays in vain for drowsy men! Pass over those who are sleeping; but what will it cost those out for a walk, those leaving the theatre in a crowd, to look at for a second and admire the brilliant constellations that radiate everywhere above their head? . . .[7]

While appropriately theoretical and idealistic when praising the magnificence of a starry night, Xavier does not hesitate to stoop to more mundane considerations. A product of the eighteenth century, he is by no means oblivious to sexuality and enlivens the narrative by coy allusions to beautiful women. What are his preferences in girl friends? Xavier magnanimously avows a love for all comely ladies: ". . . I love them all, and not only those I know or hope to meet, but all those who exist on the face of the earth. Even more, I love all the women who have existed, and those who will exist, without counting a still greater number that my imagination draws from nothingness; all possible women in short are included in the vast circle of my affections."[8]

Deftly Xavier combines the philosophical jargon of the Enlightenment and the age-old interest of all virile men in feminine pulchritude to produce rather striking results in a lightness of touch and a sprightly wit. He accomplishes this by never belaboring a point and by skipping nimbly from one topic to another. On the subject of women, he discourses glibly about famous beauties from Graeco-Roman times, Vestal Virgins and courtisans.

III *Poets and Creativity*

Xavier, ill-suited to prolonged speculations on metaphysics, is quick to change to a more insouciant mood. Poking fun at the pretentiousness of poets, a perennial target of mischievous writers, appeals to Xavier's sense of humor; he sets out to compose an *épitre*. Two questions occur to him; to whom should he address the poem and how will he go about composing the verses? "I started the project right away, and I worked for more than an hour without being able to find a rhyme for the first verse I had composed."[9]

Having hit a snag in his efforts, Xavier ponders upon the correct method of procedure to stimulate the creative faculties. The words of a great English poet come to mind, and he hastens to follow the advice of a fellow writer:

. . . I remembered then very appropriately having read somewhere that the celebrated Pope never composed anything interesting without being obliged to recite aloud for a long time and to move about in all directions in his study in order to arouse his spirits. I tried right then to imitate him. I took the poems of Ossian and recited them aloud, stalking about to raise my enthusiasm.[10]

What is a thinly veiled parody of the ridiculous posturing of some early Romantic poets could not go unnoticed. While Xavier admired Ossian, his appreciation of Macpherson's work did not keep him from taking a few frivolous liberties with the sonorous lines of the Gaelic bard. In this instance, his boisterous rendition disturbs the slumber of next door neighbors, with the result that a drowsy husband, whose pretty wife captivates the author, knocks on Xavier's door. The author, confronted by the flabbergasted gentleman, proceeds to address his nocturnal visitor in an Ossianic manner:

. . . Worthy messenger of my beautiful neighbor, I say to him in the language of the bards, why do your eyes shine under your thick brows, like two meteors in the forest of Cromba? Your beautiful companion is a ray of light, and I would die a thousand times rather than trouble her respose; but your appearance, O worthy messenger, is as somber as the most remote vault of the cavern of Camora, when the gathering clouds of the tempest obscure the moon, and bear down on the silent countryside of Morven.[11]

Xavier, far from overwhelming his perplexed visitor, only convinces the latter that he is completely insane. Unperturbed by his neighbor's hasty withdrawal and grouchy muttering, the author merely concludes that the gentleman lacks the necessary sensitivity to appreciate the charming lyricism of Ossian. Two attitudes on Xavier's part would appear to be represented here—an honest admiration of Ossian and a recognition that practical-minded persons had no patience with the vagaries of mediocre poets. A spirited army officer for whom writing was an avocation, Xavier saw the need for artists to make some personal adjustment at times to a more mundane order.

Realizing the need for a certain topicality in the *Expédition* Xavier alludes to well known persons and events. One such individual is Franz Gall, a German anatomist and founder of phrenology, who was convinced that human talents and dispositions could be ascertained with considerable accuracy by the outer appearance of the skull. Xavier alludes to Gall's findings with feigned seriousness when trying to determine the nature and actual location in the brain of man's creative faculties: ". . . I put my hand over my forehead, and I discovered a new protuberance there precisely at that part of the head where Dr. Gall placed the poetic protuberance. But I did not think about it at all then, and experience alone was to demonstrate to me the truth of the system of that famous man."[12]

The author spoofs not only poets, but also scientists, whose efforts he deems on the whole unimpressive. The "protuberance" referred to by Xavier was a bump on the head he received when colliding with the low ceiling in his flat. Bathos is employed with rather comic results as Xavier compares the merits of Pope's prescription of reading aloud to obtain inspiration and his own accidental discovery of Gall's protuberance. This venture into phrenology apparently paid off:

After having recollected a few moments in order to make one last effort in favor of my dedicatory epistle, I took a pen and started to work. What was my surprise! . . . The verses flowed by themselves from my pen, and I filled two pages in less than an hour, and I concluded from this circumstance that, if movement was necessary to Pope's head to compose verses, it took no less than a contusion to get any out ot mine. . . .[13]

If Xavier was enjoying a few moments of levity at the expense of poets, he most likely was directing his criticism at French poetry, which had produced no noteworthy outbursts of lyricism in the eighteenth century (except for André Chénier) or in the nineteenth until the *Méditations* of Lamartine in 1820. He was probably suggesting in no uncertain terms that the mediocre poets in France could, in lieu of the necessary talent, find inspiration only by receiving a blow on the head to form a "poetic protuberance." Presumably this would knock some sense into an otherwise dull and unimaginative brain. Contemporary poets also come under Xavier's purview, and he conjectures that his own poem will easily equal the befuddled efforts of second-rate hacks who have not even bothered to receive a bump on the head to compensate for an uncooperative muse:

I am so convinced in effect of the infallibility of this new method, that, in the poem of twenty-four cantos that I have composed since then, and which will be published with the *Prisoner of Pignerol*, I have not believed it necessary up to now to begin the verses; but I have written a fair copy of five hundred pages of notes, which forms, as one knows, all the merit and volume of most modern poems.[14]

The poem named by Xavier was never published, although he alludes to it elsewhere in the *Expédition*. Once he has decided to compose a poem, Xavier finds an occasion when it could be put to good use. Unfortunately, notes alone do not suffice when there is an opportunity to address fine sentiments to a fair lady on the balcony of the flat directly below his window: ". . . Finally, after having waited a long time, I believed I could risk addressing a word to her; it was only a matter of finding a compliment worthy of her and of the feelings she had inspired in me. Oh, how I regretted not having finished my dedicatory epistle in verse! How appropriately I would have used it on this occasion. . . ."[15]

No sooner does the pretty neighbor raise her head to reply to Xavier's greeting than her husband's order to retire from the balcony leaves the aspiring poet disconsolate. The Shakespearean motif of a balcony scene recalling *Romeo and Juliet* is combined with the Cinderella theme when the comely lass, in her haste to obey the order of a gruff spouse, loses a slipper while beating an abrupt retreat. Dreamily, in the fashion of lovesick poets in a decadent Neoclassical tradition, Xavier with feigned gravity expatiates on the temptation symbolized by the slipper and the dainty foot it covered:

Such was the effect of this slipper on me, without my being able to say
with certainty whether the slipper or I was the serpent, because, according
to the laws of physics, the attraction must be reciprocal. It is certain that
this deadly influence was not a trick of my imagination. I was so really and
strongly attracted that two times I was about to release my hand and
fall. . . .[16]

Mindful of the laws of physics and Newton's observations on falling bodies, Xavier discreetly abandons any wild impulse to jump
from his window to the balcony below. In spite of the thin veil of
irony pervading Xavier's remarks on poets and the creative process,
he betrays a definite insight into topics and themes that can be
readily poetized. The lady's slipper, a casual item of apparel in
itself, becomes under Xavier's facile pen the motif for some light
and graceful lines of prose on love and beauty. His more sober
reflections in other parts of the *Expédition* indicate all too well an
ability to translate commonplace subject matter into poetic concepts
developed in the flexible and pleasing style that insured the popularity of the *Voyage* and *Expédition*. Students of French literature
do well to remember that blank verse is not possible in French,
where equal stress is placed on each syllable. Only in free-flowing
prose written with rhythm and cadence can any of the effects
associated with blank verse in English be realized.

IV   *Psychological Aspects*

Disappointments, the absence of fond traveling companions, and
petulance in a fair lady, may force Xavier to eliminate any mention
of the soul and the beast, but he does not have any intention of
overlooking other ramifications of this distinction with all its psychological implications. Things in his room at the start of the second
room journey recall incidents in the first trip. "Each object recalled
to me some event of my life, and my room was covered with
souvenirs."[17] Enjoyable recollections, a pleasant feature of the
workings of memory, are replaced by more ominous mental impressions. With the arrival of nighttime, the eerie sensations produced by the gathering shadows crystalize in Xavier's active imagination as he penetrates the amorphous sphere of the dream:

I had been in bed for a quarter of an hour and, contrary to custom, I was
still not asleep. To the idea of my dedicatory epistle had succeeded the
saddest reflections; my candle, which was about to go out, cast only a

flickering and lugubrious light from the bottom of the wick, and my room looked like a tomb. A gust of wind suddenly opened the window, put out my candle, and slammed the door shut. The black tone of my thoughts increased with the darkness.[18]

Xavier's reasons for injecting a Gothic element into the narrative are understandable in light of his previous preoccupations with the workings of his own inner faculties. Descriptions of a nightmarish atmosphere do not constitute merely a convenient literary ploy, for the author is undeniably too concerned about delving into any evidence of the subconscious and the irrational. Hence, the Gothic devices used by Xavier—the wind mysteriously blowing through the room and a bat abruptly swooping down on him—must be studied cautiously. In the latter example involving the bat, while there is a seriocomic effect, Xavier's probing into the subconscious must be taken into account: ". . . A bat that was hovering around the house, and which, seeing me motionless for such a long time, apparently took me for a chimney, proceeded suddenly to beat against me and hooked on to my ear. I felt on my cheek the horrible freshness of its damp wings. All the echoes of Turin answered the furious cry I uttered in spite of myself. . . ."[19]

In a much lighter vein, Xavier sums up the prerequisites for any excursion from the wakeful state into those areas of psychological activity beyond the scope of the syllogism, where reason no longer has the final word in directing man's mental operations. The author suggests that such a procedure requires practice and is not to be undertaken lightly: ". . . It is a manner of existing that is also of my invention, and has often been of great advantage to me; but it is not granted to everyone to know how to use it; for if it is easy to give depth to one's thoughts by immersing one's self thoroughly in a subject, it is not so easy to stop one's thoughts as the pendulum of a clock is stopped. . . ."[20]

The soul-beast distinction is not needed to elucidate Xavier's point. If there are deliberate acts produced by a person's rational faculty or reason, he speculates, then there are obviously spontaneous acts as well that function uncontrolled and unregulated. The step into the irrational is willed by Xavier; but, once there, events take their course without any interference from reason which stays out of the picture. The "state of intellectual immobility" depicted by Xavier is, he admits, "voluntary and may be momentary."[21] Its close connection with sleep is all too apparent to the author, who observes the ease with which the mind shifts from one state to the other: "Since this mode of existence strongly favors the invasion of slumber, after a half minute of enjoyment I felt my head falling on my chest; I opened my eyes at once, and my ideas resumed their course, a circumstance that proves evidently that the type of voluntary lethargy involved is very different from sleep. . . ."[22]

Even though reveries or daydreams are the partly subconscious states Xavier chooses to describe, he identifies with them the oneiric phenomena associated with full-fledged dreams. Just as the steps leading up to sleep and dreaming are outlined, so are the sensations experienced on awakening recorded. The object of his dreaming in this instance is the slipper lost on the balcony below his window by a pretty neighbor:

> The brilliant vision I had just enjoyed made me feel more vividly, when I awoke, all the horror of the isolation in which I found myself. I looked all around me and saw only roofs and chimneys. Alas! Suspended on the sixth floor between heaven and earth, surrounded by an ocean of regrets, desires, and alarm, I was attached to existence only by an uncertain light of hope, a fantastic support whose fragility I had experienced too often. . . ."[23]

Inevitably, with any scrutiny of oneiric data, the questions raised by sensations of reality and unreality present themselves. Xavier's daydreams may be less horrendous than the nightmares depicted in Nodier's *Fée aux miettes;* still, the same problems confront both authors fascinated by the impressions received in dreaming. How does reality differ from unreality, and who can say with certainty that unreality, so called, is not in its way more real than what is normally termed reality? These questions plagued Nodier as they did Xavier and, in searching for an answer in the twilight zone of the subconscious, he returned to an examination of time—the measure of events in the order of their happening—so as to ascertain what factors determine the substance of objective existence. If reality, as opposed to what exists in fact outside the mind, is nothing more than the manner in which an object is represented to or perceived by the mind, then a reassessment of values, sensations, and impressions would be most necessary. This very difficulty is encountered whenever the elusive concept of time is analyzed. One aspect of time concerns the experiences associated with the temporal order. Under traumatic circumstances, time becomes distasteful when connected with unpleasant events: "O time! Terrible divinity! It is not your cruel scyth that frightens me; I only fear your hideous children, indifference and oblivion, which make a long death out of three quarters of our existence."[24]

It is only natural to seek to disprove the validity of concepts or things linked to pain and suffering. Xavier focuses on time to discern what grounds he has for rejecting it as a valid notion altogether. The various components of time upon analysis seem arbitrary, the product of caprice rather than exacting science:

> . . . In this abyss of the past, the instants and the centuries have the same length; and does the future have more reality? They are two nothings between which I am balanced as though on the edge of a blade. In truth, time seems something so inconceivable to me that I would be tempted to believe it does not really exist, and what is so named is nothing else but a punishment for thinking.[25]

To a considerable degree Xavier related his reflections on time to several fields. Their application to psychology is obvious, and from the physiological point of view he summarized some salient facts about the sensations of dreaming contrasted with the wakeful state. While his toying with conventional notions about past, present, and future could, if developed in detail, lead to a direct confrontation with established theology and even with many of the *philosophes*, Xavier refrained from any ideological debate. At any rate, he was never too far removed from orthodox thinking on the basic premises of traditional metaphysics in the Church. The implications of his interpretation of time for the creative artist represent the most revolutionary conclusion to be drawn from Xavier's observations. He is capable of taking a Romantic commonplace, the tolling of a bell as a reminder of the limited span of man's days on earth, and converting it into a whimsical commentary on temporal existence:

> . . . In vain the prophetic voice of the bell announces to them the approach of eternity; in vain it repeats to them sadly each hour that has just flowed by; they hear nothing, or, if they hear, they do not understand. O midnight! Terrible hour! I am not superstitious, but this hour always inspired in me a kind of fear, and I have the presentiment that, if ever I were to come to die, it would be at midnight. . . .[26]

Familiar strains from Chateaubriand's *Génie du Christianisme* come to mind as Xavier meditates on the tolling of the bell. Usually in the *Expédition* he endeavors to dismiss weighty subjects with a few gay, tongue-in-cheek remarks. The far-reaching conclusions of his comments on momentous questions such as time are, however, inescapable. His rather Poe-esque reaction to the sound of a bell is that of the *litterateur* who, elsewhere in the *Expédition*, clearly indicates his awareness of the artistic possibilities of drawing upon expanded concepts of time for fresh literary themes. What Xavier proposes is actually an elaboration in somewhat greater detail of Joseph's observations on time and its future impact on artists and poets in the *Soirées de Saint-Pétersbourg*.

V   *Feminine Ideal*

Time and again in the *Voyage* and *Expédition* Xavier returns to the motif of the feminine ideal. As a rule his contemplation of a particular fair lady is carried out in a manner more suggestive of an oneiric than of a wakeful atmosphere. These encounters with comely lasses occur at odd and unexpected moments. After having scarcely terminated one meditation, he discovers himself in an elegant company where the center of attraction is a beautiful woman about whom he has dreamed before:

> . . . Recovering suddenly like a sleepy man on whom a bucket of water would be tossed, I perceived that several people had surrounded me to examine me while my enthusiasm was causing me to talk to myself. I then saw the beautiful Georgine who was a few steps ahead of me. Half of her red cheek covered with rouge, which I saw through the hair of her blond wig, finally put me in touch with the affairs of this world, from which I had just been absent for a brief period.[27]

The chief elements in the passage at hand bear a striking similarity once again to the gossamery visions of the feminine ideal that alternately appear and fade away through Nerval's writings. Xavier is no longer dealing with the static model of feminine pulchritude fashioned along Classical lines. She has already become the Romantic woman, magnified by those writers who add to her dimensions the amorphous yet ethereal imagery of the dream world. Nodier in the *Fée aux miettes* beholds several facets of the same woman in the fairy as the Queen of Sheba and the jolly, goodnatured hag. Xavier's ideal by Nervalean standards is more sophisticated in conception, for like Gérard he catches tantalizing and repeated glimpses of various feminine exemplars. Some are haughty and elusive and others upbraid the author for some imagined wrong. In the case of Xavier, Mme de Hautcastel scolds him for not presenting a sufficient number of love scenes in the *Voyage,* and he tries to remedy the situation gracefully in the *Expédition:* " . . . She could not make the same reproach to this new trip; and, although my adventure with my fair neighbor was not pursued further, I can affirm I found more satisfaction there than in any other circumstance, where I had imagined myself to be very happy, for want of any point of comparison. . . ."[28] Xavier's desire to clarify the reader's understanding of the *raison d'être* for this quest of a feminine ideal obliges him to leave no stone unturned in presenting a lucid exposition of the procedure followed. His explanation to Mme de Hautcastel is a concise resumé of his aim and purpose in treating this particular theme: " . . . Yes, madam, I love them all, and not only those that I know or hope to meet, but all those that exist on the face of the earth. Even more, I love all the women who have existed, and those who will exist, without counting a much greater number that my imagination draws from nothingness; all the women possible are included, in short, in the vast circle of my affections."[29]

Caution must be exercised of course to avoid drawing any undue conclusions from Xavier's statement. He does not, on one hand, outline in detail the course to be followed in exploring oneiric phenomena and in the dream-quest of the ideal woman by future writers like Nerval. On the other hand, he unmistakably is in the process of developing a literary device to be used by the Romantics. His ideas are at the stage to be expected in a precursor with the ingenuity and foresight to envision developments that will transpire in coming literary generations. In many respects Xavier was more advanced in this aspect of his thinking than Lamartine and other writers of the first phase of Romanticism. With the exception of Nodier, only writers of the second phase, Nerval and Baudelaire, would enlarge upon the themes proposed by Xavier.

VI   *Solitude and Nature*

Several themes of the *Voyage* are recapitulated in the *Expédition nocturne,* among them those concerning solitude and nature. In a pre-Baudelairean vein, Xavier reflects on the problems confronting a person seeking solitude in an urban society. A more mature view is expressed in the *Expédition;* solitude has its attractions, but man cannot lose sight of the responsibilities of being a gregarious creature:

I will still confess, I love solitude in big cities; but, unless forced there by some grave circumstance like a trip around my room, I only wish to be a hermit in the morning; in the evening I like to see human faces again. The drawbacks of social life and those of solitude destroy each other, and these two modes of existence are embellished by one another.[30]

The rather relaxed manner in which Xavier reconciles himself to the necessity of balancing a daily schedule with some periods spent alone and others in the company of friends does not imply that moments of solitude have lost their original appeal to him. He still responds wholeheartedly to the physical beauty of hills, trees, and flowers. A spot near his residence offers welcome refuge from cares and frustrations: "Charming hill! You have seen me search again for your solitary retreats and prefer your sequestered paths to the bright walks of the capital; you have often seen me lost in your labyrinths of verdure, attentive to the song of the early pigeon, with my heart full of a vague restlessness and with the burning desire to fix myself forever in your enchanted valleys. . . ."[31]

Xavier's awareness of nature is that of a social being, the product of a refined culture, not a crude cenobite. The lingering influence of Ossian and *La Nouvelle Héloïse* kept him sensitized to the physical world about him. His momentary lyrical effusions represent a pose in part, but a spontaneous reaction as well. In many of these passages depicting subjective responses to nature found in Romantic literature two factors have to be taken into account, the writer's observance of certain conventions expected of him by the reader and his own genuine reactions. Xavier handles these Romantic impulses with a nice sense of Classical restraint. An endless flow of vocabulary in the manner of Hugo would be foreign to his temperament. From this standpoint Xavier is much closer to Lamartine's subdued and elegant style in communing with nature.

When speaking of Xavier's affinity to Lamartine in their mutual approach to the physical world, its wonders and beauties, mention should be made of the love of all creation they mutually espoused. Both writers felt a vital principle existed in all creation and was reflected to an extent even in the allegedly inanimate order of minerals and plants. Xavier expresses an overflowing love not only for humanity but all parts of God's creation—a concept almost Hinduistic in its implications:

Outside of the half of the human species for whom I have a deep affection, shall I say it and will I be believed? My heart is endowed with such a capacity for tenderness, that all living beings and inanimate things themselves are also a good part of it. I love the trees that lend me their shade, and the birds that twitter under their foliage, and the nocturnal cry of the owl, and the noise of the torrents; I love all . . . I love the moon![32]

The depth of Xavier's feelings about nature, voiced in the *Expédition*, is stated with heartfelt conviction in the closing pages. Two aspects of nature, in a larger sense, greet him: the city constructed by human hands and the physical glories God alone could create. Tormented by his inability to record the emotions he undergoes, Xavier gives vent nonetheless to the profound sensations he experiences at the sight of surroundings so dear to him. The simplicity and directness of the description mark this passage as one of the high points of the *Expédition:*

> . . . Never had the night appeared so beautiful to me; never had the spectacle before my eyes interested me so vividly. After having bade farewell to the mountain and the church of Superga, I took leave of the towers, the bell-towers, all the known objects that I would never have believed I could miss so much, and of the air and the sky and of the river whose murmur seemed to answer my adieux. Oh! If I only knew how to picture the sentiment, at once tender and cruel, that filled my heart. . . .[33]

Xavier's attitude toward nature betrays the poetic side of his temperament. Unlike Joseph, he was less inclined to be the ideologue and took a more intimate view of the outside world. The former was too engrossed in philosophy, theology, and political science to rhapsodize about scenes of exquisite natural beauty. Xavier, while affected by the turmoil of the French Revolution, sought outlets for his emotions more overtly than Joseph did. The younger brother was in this respect more Romantic in mood and temperament.

VII   *The Sky Motif*

Closely connected with Xavier's fondness for nature was his preoccupation with the sky and stars. So much was Xavier involved with the grandeur of the heavens that it constitutes a separate theme in the *Expédition*. His earlier participation in balloon ascensions doubtless increased his love of the sky and outer space. In his garret flat, owing to its location on the top floor, Xavier had only to look out the window to see the sky: "The closest external objects that met my eyes were the moon and the morning star, which placed me in immediate rapport with the sky."[34]

Memories of the exultation sensed in the successful balloon ascension at Chambéry apparently had a lasting effect, revealed in his fascination with the heavens and infinity. Xavier is mesmerized by anything recapturing the sensations of soaring into the empyrean. The stepladder leading up to the window in his room intrigues Xavier and he takes delight in mounting it at the slightest provocation. Similarly, the flight of migratory birds overhead invokes admiration and envy in the author:

> . . . I saw them cross the sky from cloud to cloud. "Ah! How well they fly!" I whispered. "With what confidence they seem to glide over the invincible path they traverse!" I shall confess it! Alas! May I be pardoned! The horrible feeling of envy entered my heart for one single time, and it was because of the cranes. I followed them with my jealous eyes to the very limits of the horizon. . . .[35]

To Xavier the sky has several facets; this wonder of nature does not appear one-sided to him. One minute he is overcome with the aeronaut's desire to travel in space and the next he is absorbed in a revery, oblivious to all about him save the placid beauty of the starry sky:

> The weather was serene, the Milky Way like a light cloud partitioned off the sky, a soft ray left each star to come right to me, and when I examined one attentively, its companions seemed to sparkle more brightly to attract my gaze.
> It is always a fresh delight for me to contemplate the starry sky, and I don't have to reproach myself for making one single trip, or even a simple walk at night, without paying the tribute of admiration that I owe to the marvels of the firmament.[36]

The more serious aspect of Xavier's preoccupation with the sky is discernible when he beholds in it a symbol of eternity and the immortality of the human spirit. In a passage that seems an echo of the vague deism of many writers of a Rousseauistic persuasion, Xavier strives to penetrate the mystery behind the cosmic forces represented by the stars and other heavenly bodies:

> Brilliant star! I exclaimed in the enjoyable ecstasy that ravished me, incomprehensible product of eternal thought! You, who alone motionless in the heavens, watch over a half of the earth since the day of creation! You, who direct the navigator on the lonely expanses of the ocean, and of whom the sight alone has returned hope and life to the sailor harrassed by the tempest! . . .[37]

Xavier unequivocally states his belief in a personal God, "a divine providence who guides men by unknown means." It is important to note that the author generally endeavors to balance the intellective and intuitive, or irrational, functions of his mind. This is especially true when he is engaged in contemplating the stars or some similar object of a profound meditation. Prior to preparing himself for an intellectual analysis of the physical forces in the universe, he has a moment of relaxation when temporarily all mental activity is halted and the instinctual operations of the psyche are readied to enjoy the beauties of nature. Without question Xavier conscientiously strives to clarify for himself and the reader precisely what he is doing and the procedure he follows: " . . . During the interval of rest that I had just enjoyed, my imagination had recovered all its strength, and my heart was ready to receive the fairest impressions; how this temporary suppression of mental activity can increase its energy! . . .[38]

Some remarks on Xavier bear repeating. One such observation is a reminder that he was torn between conflicting ideological loyalties. Catholicism, despite stages of indifference he may have experienced common to many church members, was always a strong factor in determining his religious and philosophical outlook. The Enlightenment still left its mark on Xavier and he mouthed some of the clichés of the *philosophes* from time to time. Without becoming a dyed-in-the-wool rationalist, he was open-minded and accepted certain features of the *philosophes'* inquiries into and comments on psychology, physiology, and other sciences, particularly in relation to man's mental and emotional functions. These questions are interwoven through the fabric of the *Voyage* and the *Expédition*.

VIII   *Politics in the* Expédition

When plucking petals from a daisy to determine whether a certain lady loved him or not, Xavier's thoughts turn unaccountably to the shocking events currently taking place in Europe and above all in France. Although nations foresee their days are numbered, they still go at each other's throats and civil turmoil and rebellion cause the death of innocent persons:

> . . . Conquerors, dragged along themselves by the rapid whirlwind of time, enjoy casting thousands of men down on the pavement. Gentlemen! What are you thinking about? Wait! These good people were going to die in due time. Do you not see the wave advancing? It is already foaming near the shore. Wait, in the name of heaven, just one moment, and you, and your enemies, and I . . . all that is going to end! Can one be sufficiently amazed at such madness! Come now, that is one point decided; henceforth, I will no longer pluck any daisies.[39]

Xavier shares on more than one occasion Joseph's grim vision of the current crisis in Europe. He does not delve as deeply as his older brother into the underlying causes, but arrives, nonetheless, at essentially the same conclusion. Europe, poisoned by the heretical preachments of the *philosophes*, is suffering from the reckless overthrow of legitimate authority residing in the throne and altar. Once the restraints necessary for a peaceful society are rejected, chaos is inevitable.

Recognizing that nationalism is at the root of many wars, Xavier investigates those factors that are decisive in determining a citizen's love of country and devotion to its regime: "I soon saw that love of the fatherland depends on several elements joined together, that is to say the enduring habit acquired by man, since his childhood, from individuals, locality, and government. It was only a question of examining in what way these three bases contribute, each for its part, to making up the fatherland."[40]

Like Joseph, Xavier had no qualms about using Montesquieu's thinking if it served to clarify problems in political science. Little effort was required to Christianize any *philosophe,* especially Montesquieu, to make good use of salient features in his philosophy. In this case, Montesquieu's emphasis on the environment as a capital influence in forming the attitude of citizens in a particular commonwealth is accepted unhesitatingly by Xavier. The latter realizes that high-sounding talk about intangibles, such as loyalty and religion, can only go so far in explaining devotion to a particular region. Obviously, other causes must be assessed to obtain a complete picture of a very complex process:

Locality contributes for as least as much to the attachment we have to our native country. On this subject a very interesting question arises; at all times it has been noticed that mountaineers are, of all people, those who are the most attached to their country, and that nomad people live in general on great plains. What can be the cause of this difference in the attachment of these people to the region? If I am not mistaken, here it is: in the mountains the fatherland has a face; in the plains it does not have any at all. It is a woman without a face one could not love, in spite of all her good qualities. . . .[41]

Nationalism and devotion to country were traits translated into literary themes by Romantic poets, novelists, and playwrights. Periodically in the *Voyage* and *Expédition* Xavier touches on subjects relating to Romanticism as though he felt it his task to sum up the major intellectual and artistic trends of his time. The topic of nationalism was very appropriate. Montesquieu analyzed it in the *Esprit des lois*, and the upsurge of patriotic fervor in France excited first by the Revolution and later by Napoleon's conquests made it a burning issue in Xavier's period. The author himself was driven out of his own country and exiled as a result of the excessive nationalism and subsequent expansionism that arose in France. Continuing in his application of Montesquieu's principles to the current state of affairs in Europe, Xavier concludes that the character of a given country depends on its guiding principle: "Is the government good? The fatherland is in its full power. Is it becoming vicious? The fatherland is sick. Is it changing? Is it dying? It is then a new fatherland, and each one has the power to adopt or choose another."[42]

No extensive analysis is necessary to judge what Xavier's feelings in the matter were. He had seen the tatterdemalion regiments of revolutionary France chase out the rightful ruler of Sardinia. If some Sardinians wished to stay and form a democracy, the modern equivalent of a people's republic, they were welcome to that choice. Xavier's course was clear. A voluntary exile in Russia was the only alternative to an immoral compromise.

Comments on politics and revolution made by Xavier are invariably a direct reflection of Joseph's opinion. They also prefigure what would prove to be motifs in the writings of French Romanticism. The social views of Lamartine and Hugo, affected by the French Revolution and Bonapartism, were echoed in their poems. George Sand selected democracy and revolution as themes central to many of her novels. Dumas *père* in his plays and novels frequently used the turbulent 1790's and 1800s as the basis for a plot and story line.

IX *Sensibility in the* Voyage *and* Expédition

Sensibility is a term usually applied to a movement or tendency in eighteenth century French literature. Among its exponents were writers of the caliber of Rousseau and Diderot. In these two authors sensibility was generally treated as a faculty that transcended the rather plodding functions of reason to present an immediate and higher order of knowledge to the intellect. Sensibility thus had a preeminent role in the operations of the mind. Reason, relegated to the area of analysis through the syllogism, was unable to satisfy certain needs and desires, and the habitual restlessness of a highly sensitive and perceptive individual. This affective aspect of the soul, the emotional response to pleasurable or unpleasurable aspects of the mental process, did not go unchallenged by hardcore Classicists and rationalists; it went against the grain. They were not ready to concede that sensibility was a function worthy of serious study, being too subjective and illogical. Defenders of sensibility replied that there was indisputably in certain individuals, artists in particular, a highly developed acuteness of apprehension. Readily affected by external influences, sensibility was often expressed in a keen consciousness of the outside world as well as a sensitive awareness of man's inner functions. Responsiveness and susceptibility to external stimuli were manifested especially in the artist's capacity to draw effortlessly intellective and esthetic distinctions. The latter were invariably the product of intuition and not of a laborious analysis.

The debate in French intellectual circles has continued well into the twentieth century. Artistic movements that stress sensibility and intuition, like Romanticism and Symbolism, draw the fire of more objectively oriented critics distrustful of what they deem undue emphasis on an at best vague and amorphous concept of the creative process.[43]

Supporters of sensibility reply that the good effects of the movement far outweigh the bad. Readings of descriptive poetry and dramatic scenes from sentimental novels and plays in eighteenth century salons provided the occasion, it is true, for ridiculous posturing and foolish displays of emotion but there was more to the movement than that. Sensibility had a very serious side. Rather than weakening man's moral fiber, for example, sensibility strengthened it by making the public more responsive to misery and suffering, something not accomplished by cold rationalism alone.

Areas other than moral awareness were investigated in the eighteenth century thanks to the current of sensibility. The complexity of man's bodily and emotional functions was studied in all its ramifications—physical, psychological, and physiological. Sensibility in the physical sphere dealt with theories on the origin of life and movement, in the psychological with the mental and emotional operations of the mind, and in the physiological with the function of living organisms and their parts. Of the leading *philosophes,* Diderot, more than the others, explored in greater depth the implications of sensibility in all of the three categories outlined above; he also defined the workings of the esthetic sensibility in fine arts.

Sensibility, thus understood, is a rather extensive topic and the proper object of ongoing research in an unending examination of its multifaceted implications. Its application to Xavier de Maistre is appropriate inasmuch as the *Voyage* and *Expédition* were catchalls for many current fads and notions in politics, art, science, philosophy, and religion. Sensibility was no exception and, while it had its strongest manifestations in the eighteenth century, the lingering effects of the movement were felt in the nineteenth among the Romantics. Lamartine exhibited many of its symptoms in his esthetic and emotional responses and George Sand in her social novels portrayed the keen consciousness of moral and societal wrongs in her sensitive characters. As part of the general picture of French Romanticism, Xavier de Maistre evinced a more than passing exposure to sensibility.

In the *Expédition* Xavier outlines the basic conflict between the two opposing forces in man, intellectual and intuitional. Invariably he finds himself in a quandary when trying to determine which faculty proposes the best course of action: "The head and heart of man, I exclaimed, then, are two strange machines! Carried along in turn by these principles of his actions, in two opposite directions, the last that he follows always seems the best to him! O madness of enthusiasm and sentiment! says cold reason; O weakness and uncertainty of reason! says sentiment. Who will ever be able, who will decide between them?"[44]

Eighteenth century thought again leaves its mark on Xavier in the reference to two important faculties as machines. This mechanistic aspect, covering only the physiological side of sensibility, is balanced by a recognition of psychological considerations. The two drives in man, struggling for control, are presented by Xavier as a continuous process never reaching a definitive solution. The soul-beast relationship depicted in the *Voyage* is in all probability an offshoot of the endless controversy over the issues raised by the vogue of sensibility. In the *Expédition* and *Voyage* Xavier treats some of the main features of the movement.

Besides the philosophical implications of sensibility, Xavier touches on some of its more conventional features encountered in novels, plays, and poems. A seemingly insignificant incident becomes meaningful when Xavier is deeply affected by Prévost's *Cleveland* and proceeds to cry softly. Such was the accepted function, nonetheless, of a novel conforming to the canons of sensibility. By this token the successful writer was one who obliged the reader to identify with the main character's perils and tribulations. The tearful passages of *Cleveland* had an obliging participant in Xavier: "Finally, I enter so much into his troubles, I take such great interest in him and his unfortunate family that the unexpected appearance of the ferocious *Ruintons* makes my hair stand on end; a cold sweat covers me when I read this passage and my fright is as vivid, as real as if I were to be roasted myself and eaten by this mob."[45]

Xavier observed the rules on courtly and chivalrous conduct when describing the theme of the feminine ideal and went to some lengths to show his awareness of this prominent part of sensibility. He defends the manner in which he approaches his pretty neighbor in the *Expé*dition and is determined not to have readers misinterpret his conduct: " . . . I will prove to them that, if I had indulged in banter on this important occasion, I would have openly failed the rules of prudence and good taste. Every man who enters into conversation with a beautiful lady by telling a joke or paying a compliment, however flattering he may be, allows ambitions to be revealed which are supposed to appear only when they are beginning to be justified. . . . "[46]

Xavier draws some delicate distinctions that savor of the refined code of sensibility and preciosity as well. He gently inquires into the emotions and motives that come into play when a gentleman courts the attention of a comely maid of good breeding. Reason is relegated to second place and the sublimated insights born of sensibility guide the gentleman in the right path; he has only to cooperate. Xavier is painstaking in his efforts to convince readers that his behavior is above reproach even when imagining what he would do if called upon to assuage the apprehensions of a woman in distress: "What sweet and melancholy enjoyment would not a sensitive man experience in approaching this unfortunate one to console her!"[47]

In his delightful encounters with beautiful women in his dreams and reveries, Xavier recognizes the symptoms of sensibility. They consist of certain traits that are especially manifest in the feminine character: "Unhappy beauties have in particular rights over my heart, and the tribute of sensibility that I owe them does not weaken at all the interest I have in those who are happy. This disposition varies my pleasure infinitely, and permits me to pass in turn from melancholy to gaiety, and from a sentimental repose to exultation."[48]

What Xavier delineates is a few stages of sensibility that may concern a casual, or somewhat more intimate, relationship between the sexes. Through the veneer of drawing room etiquette can be seen a temperament quite responsive to the misfortunes of others. This compassionate side of Xavier's disposition, also one of the many components of sensibility, is demonstrated in his sorrow at having treated Joannetti harshly. The occasion was a scolding the valet accepted in humble silence for not having a brush to dust and polish the master's shoes. "May heaven bless him! Philosophers! Christians! Have you read?" Such was Xavier's reaction as he realized in shame that the servant had taught him a much needed object lesson. After Joannetti leaves to purchase a brush, Xavier manifests the spirit of contrition expected in an advocate of sensibility. "I took the cloth and I briskly cleaned my left shoe, on which I shed a tear of repentance."[49] When Joannetti leaves his service to get married, Xavier has further reflections on the rewarding association with the kind and generous nature of human relationships: " . . . A few minutes have sufficed to make strangers to one another two old companions for fifteen years. O sad, sad condition of humanity, never being able to find a single stable object on which to place the least of his affections!"[50]

One of the most moving passages in the *Voyage*, and the most heartfelt manifestation of sensibility, is Xavier's unaffected and sincere tribute to his deceased father. Much insight is afforded as well into the depth of the family ties fostered in the Maistre household. The conservative and religious atmosphere engendered a strong and thoroughly masculine relationship between father and son, but one still characterized by profound affection: Xavier is comforted by the thought that his father was spared the sight of the French invasion and the devastating effect on the Maistres:

> . . . How many evils would a longer life have made you experience! O my father! Is the fate of your numerous family known to you in the sojourn of happiness? Do you know that your children are exiled from this country that you served for sixty years with so much zeal and integrity? Do you know that they are forbidden to visit your tomb? But tyranny has been unable to erase the most precious part of your heritage—the memory of your virtues and the strength of your example. . . .[51]

By honoring the memory of a beloved parent with simple eloquence, Xavier accomplishes the union of heart and mind, the two faculties usually, by his own definition, in continual conflict. Sensibility for Xavier is not always a frivolous convention, a useful literary ploy with which to beguile the reader. Rather, it is in its

most serious form the honest manifestation of a profound concern
for the deeper values in life: friendship, charity, and love. As
manifested in Xavier's Christian fellow feeling for others, it recalls
the concept of the *honnête homme* in the seventeenth century—often defined as an individual whose personal traits ex-
emplified the best teachings of Christianity.

Many elements in the tribute paid to Xavier's father are decidedly Romantic, above all the nostaglic invocation of the past and
evidence of regression, the desire to return to the less complicated
period of life associated with childhood. The *Voyage* and *Expédition* on this basis serve as an example of the manner in which
eighteenth century sensibility provided a link with the Romantic
movement in the nineteenth.

CHAPTER 4

Le Lépreux de la cité d'Aoste

I *Background and Summary*

Le Lépreux was published in Saint Petersburg in 1811 without mention of Xavier as the author. The story is based on Xavier's friendship with a leper. The dramatic dialogue transpires in the city of Aosta in Piedmont. Xavier describes the southern section of the city as it was in the eighteenth century, bordering on open fields and enjoying the charm of the countryside. Ancient ruins dating from Roman times and the Middle Ages remained, and were the subject of popular legends. A landmark in the area was the Tour de la Frayeur, reportedly inhabited by ghosts. Old women testified that they had seen an apparition, a lady in white holding a lamp. Connected with an ancient wall and constructed in marble, the tower had been repaired fifteen years before, by the governor's decree, to house a leper and prevent him from spreading the dread malady. The leper was left largely to his own resources and periodically provided by the townspeople with food and garden implements. Except for an occasional visit by a workman delivering provisions or by a priest the leper lived in solitude. During fighting in the Alps in 1797 a soldier, in reality Xavier, happened to pass by and out of curiosity entered the garden to surprise the leper in the midst of a midday reverie. The somber man warns the unexpected visitor to leave, but, on hearing the kind reassurances of the soldier, invites him to stay at his own risk.

Against this background the dialogue in which the leper relates a pathetic and heart-rending story begins. He confides to the visitor that the sound of a human voice alone is an immeasurable consolation and a welcome relief from a daily routine whose high point consists in tending the garden and inspecting the flowers. What follows is the leper's description of his plight and the struggle to overcome his despair.

II *Religious Themes*

There are variations to the religious themes in *Le Lépreux*. What would appear to be limited in its theological implications actually goes much more deeply into the problems underlying the human condition, for the tale deals with life and death in a vale of tears. Xavier makes an apt choice in using a victim of leprosy to develop religious motifs of great significance to him since they vividly reflect his own misery in seeing home and family uprooted by the French Revolution.

Time can have different effects on persons depending on their situation. To the leper the passing of time has a religious meaning since somehow, despite its snaillike pace, it can still move forward at a rate that placates even the most wretched: "Ills and sorrows make the hours seem long, but the years still flow by with the same rapidity. At the ultimate point of misfortune there is still a joy the average man cannot know, and which will appear very singular to you, that of existing and breathing. . . ."[1]

The temporal aspect of man's existence on earth is a recurrent theme in spiritual writers and the leper, with the *Bible* and the *Imitation of Christ* at his disposal, is aware of the implications of the passing of time and the need to appreciate simple joys. Such an attitude is more often anticipated in a monk, but the leper is leading in effect a conventual life. His adaptability becomes understandable when the religious themes in Xavier's tale bring out the monastic frame of mind that prompts his actions. A long-standing practice in monasteries, custody of the eyes, is scrupulously observed by brother and sister. Their immediate reason in not looking at each other is to avoid the painful sight of their mutual disfigurement: ". . . When we came together to pray to God, we kept from looking at each other, for fear that the sight of our afflictions might disturb our meditations, and our glances dared be reunited only in heaven. After our prayers my sister usually retired to her cell or under the hazels at the end of the garden, and we almost always lived separated from each other."[2]

The importance of allowing nothing to distract their prayers is part of the total picture in *Le Lépreux*, where acceptance of the divine will is paramount. A spirit of resignation is bolstered by prayer, and for the Romantic, even one of the leper's orthodox stripe, no better lessons in forebearance are to be read than those taught in the Book of Job; in its pages the leper discovers a never failing source of consolation: "More tranquil I went up to my room. I used the rest of the night to read the Book of Job, and the holy enthusiasm that it caused to pass into my soul ended by dissipating entirely the dark thoughts that had obsessed me. . . ."[3]

Fortified by his reading of Job, the leper is able to meet the ultimate challenge: death at the end of what seems infinite suffering. Unlike more worldly counterparts in Romantic literature, the leper accepts Job's words of advice at face value and does not distort them to accommodate and justify his own frustrations and melancholy. None of these discordant elements enter into the religious themes of *Le Lépreux*. Xavier has no time or patience for self-pity; the latter is readily explainable in the leper in view of his condition, which even then is overcome by studying the example of Job. Resignation to what God has in store is the ultimate message and motif in *Le Lépreux*. The occasion for the leper's process of atonement and purification is in the death of his sister. Her last days remain an inspiring model to him of submission to the Almighty: "Her tenderness had made her afraid of troubling me; but she came to be close enough to help me. I heard her reciting the *Miserere* softly. I knelt down near the door, and, without interrupting her, I followed her words in my mind. My eyes were full of tears; who would not have been touched by such affection? . . ."[4]

Xavier does not avoid Romantic scenes if they are susceptible of an orthodox interpretation. The sister dying in her brother's arms is intensely human and entirely believable, given the fact of the two lepers' piety and faithful practice of their religion. Although the brother weakened previously at one point, he now finds the strength to attend her calmly in her last moments without lapsing into hysteria: " . . . 'Pass into eternity, my dear sister!' I said to her. 'Free yourself from life; leave this body in my arms.' For three hours I held her thus in the last struggle of life; she passed away gently, and her soul disengaged itself from the earth effortlessly."[5]

The leper is now in a position to spend the remainder of his time on earth with complete acquiescence in God's plans. He tells the soldier of his sister's final message to him contained in a letter written just before her demise:

My brother, soon I am going to leave you, but I will not abandon you. From heaven, where I hope to go, I will watch over you; I will pray to God that he may give you the courage to endure life with resignation, until it pleases him to unite us in another world; then I will be able to show you all my affection. . . .[6]

The crux of the theological point being emphasized by Xavier is summed up by the sister. Suffering on earth for the Christian has meaning, especially when loved ones who have shared the same misfortunes die and then intercede in heaven for those still remaining on earth. His sister's death prefigures to the leper his own, and in her letter is a basic concept that reinforces the theme underlying *Le Lépreux*, that prayer and suffering are efficacious and pleasing to God. Xavier has selected the love of brother and sister, from which sexuality is absent, to illustrate his point. As an alternative to the carnal love with a superficial Christian veneer so popular in Romantic writings, Xavier proposes a love chaste and simple in character and in conformity with Christian teaching.

III   *The Leper's View of Nature*

Another commonplace in French Romantic literature was the description of nature, the physical forces at work in the universe. Interpretations could vary from an orderly décor of well-trimmed gardens and symmetrical wooded groves to a dynamic vision of majestic mountains and tremendous oceans that vigorously indicated the presence of a powerful Providence in control of creation. Xavier opted for a serene interpretation of nature on the leper's part and one oriented toward a respectful acquiescence in the divine will. There was no place in Xavier's scheme of things for an angry, defiant hero hurling blasphemy after blasphemy at the rivers and trees as though to settle a score with God.

The leper has a structured view of nature in keeping with the resignation he has adopted as a way of life. With this resignation there is the quiet resolution to comply with the advice in the *Imitation of Christ* to cherish a refuge from the world. In accord with these principles, the leper admires nature and does what he can to cultivate the garden and plants around his abode: "The trees are still young; I have planted them myself, as well as this vine that I have trained to climb right on top of the old wall there, and whose width forms a little walk for me; it is my favorite spot."[7]

As might be expected, the orderliness the leper realizes, literally in his own backyard by attending to the plants and trees, is indicative of a generally disciplined outlook on nature. With his thoughts focused on eternity, the leper is attracted more to the broader aspects of nature, the changing of the seasons and the weather, the inalterable magnificence of the fields and hills. He lacks the restlessness of the impulsive and uneasy poet:

. . . I spend whole days in fine weather motionless on this rampart, enjoying the air and the beauty of nature; all my ideas then are vague, indeterminate; sadness reposes in my heart without overwhelming it; my eyes wander about this countryside and the crags which surround us; these different aspects are so imprinted in my memory that they are, so to speak, part of myself, and each site is a friend I see with pleasure everyday.[8]

Although beholding individual objects and locations with a feeling of intimacy, the leper stops short of animating them to the point that their voices can be heard in reply. If the leper senses a certain dynamism in the flora and elements above him, he does so only to the extent that they mirror the eternal life-giving power of God. What is of paramount importance to the leper is the spiritual awakening he undergoes whenever he has the opportunity to study carefully the panorama viewed from the tower:

. . . Although the power of God is as visible in the creation of an ant as in that of the entire universe, the grand spectacle of the mountains makes a greater impression on my senses; I cannot see these enormous masses covered with eternal ice without experiencing a religious amazement, but, in this vast tableau that surrounds me, I have favorite sites I prefer; among them is the hermitage you see up there on the summit of the mountain of Charvensod. Isolated in the middle of the woods, it receives the last rays of the setting sun. . . .[9]

Xavier most often is a visual writer, a trait linked to his painting. Here the author, speaking through the leper, selects those features of a panorama pleasing to an artist's eye. The perspective of the leper is to be anticipated in a deeply religious person. It should be noted that the fact of God's omnipotence is accepted without question and is witnessed by the leper in "religious amazement," key words that suggest a form of ecstasy, an experience common to mystics. There is no room here for wild, discursive reflections on the origin and purpose of creation. The humble leper has no desire or inclination to demand an explanation of God for the injustice in the world. This is the function of the skeptical *homme fatal*, not the convinced Christian.

If there is an association of human concerns with physical objects, it is done gently and modestly without any undue display of emotion. A few signs that formerly indicated his sister's presence are now absent since her death. With a Classical simplicity, and mention only of the essential details, Xavier explains how the leper's memories are stirred by the natural setting about him:

. . . In the evening when I was watering my garden, she strolled sometimes in the setting sun, here at the very spot where I am talking to you, and I saw her shadow passing and repassing on my flowers. Even when I did not see her, I found traces everywhere of her presence. Now I no longer happen to find on my path a flower with the petals plucked off or some branches of a shrubby tree she dropped when passing by. . . .[10]

When despondent over the passing of his sister, the leper is in no mood to appreciate the happiness of others. The sound of merry voices in the woods near the tower angers him. Contented people, in a nature suddenly become complacent and indifferent, represent to the leper the injustice in the world when pleasure can coexist with extreme sorrow: "I heard the indistinct murmur of joy; I saw between the trees the brilliant colors of their clothes, and this entire group seemed surrounded by a cloud of happiness. I could not stand this spectacle; the torments of hell had entered my heart; I looked away and ran back to my cell. . . ."[11]

Contrary to the prescribed modus operandi of the *homme fatal*, the leper does not sit and mope in a secluded corner of the tower or brood about the best method of suicide: a rope or poison. He may give vent to understandably human impulses, but not for long. Capable of surmounting the temptation to kill himself, he does not blame nature for his woes, and discovers instead the solace he is seeking in a starlight sky, a scene reminiscent of the *Expédition:* " . . . Never had the firmament appeared so serene and so beautiful; a star was shining before my window; I contemplated it for a long time with an indescribable pleasure, thanking God for having granted me the joy of seeing it, and I felt a secret consolation in thinking that somehow one of its rays was destined for the sad cell of the leper."[12]

Unrequited love of the typical Romantic variety could not allow this sort of ending; if it were a happy one, lovers would be reunited after countless tribulations to enjoy in full view of a glorious panorama an earthly paradise of sensual delights. The *homme fatal* would see this promise disappear before his eyes and curse the stars for their indifference to human suffering and the heartless deity who created them. At the termination of many cruel tests of his faith, Xavier's Christian *homme fatal* achieves a peace unknown to this world and a glimpse of the reward in store; to the leper the firmament is a foretoken of the beatific vision when the true believer meets God face to face. Individual reactions to a setting of great natural beauty do depend on the beholder's state of mind.

IV   *The Christine* homme fatal

The *Lépreux de la cité d'Aoste* differs strongly in tone and viewpoint from the Byronism rampant in Lamartine and many other French Romantic poets such as Hugo and Musset. The Byronic pattern for the *homme fatal* was the handsome, sensitive individual misunderstood by society and standing on a rocky slope overlooking the ocean with his long locks flowing in the wind. This was a melodramatic portrait indeed and one associated with a particular manifestation of Romanticism. Byron was not the property of poets alone but also of some rather cynical prosateurs. Stendhal and Mérimée, for varying reasons, admired the English writer as a symbol of the superior man who did not cater to bourgeois norms. Their Byron was not an emotionally sick person, but a rugged individualist scornful of society's arbitrary conventions.

Xavier was already prepared to propose an alternative to the *homme fatal,* since he had criticized the emotional instability of Werther and the inordinate subjectivism of modern writers. He supported the basic teachings of Catholicism and consequently sought an ideal in keeping with the austerity preached in the *Imitation of Christ* and the Book of Job; the famous episode in the Old Testament was looked upon by many Romantics as a prototype of lyric melancholy and pessimism. When viewed from the stern viewpoint of orthodox Christianity, the Book of Job is an object lesson in man's sinfulness and a treatise on the need of repentance for salvation.

Far from being a dashing hero, it is a humble and solitary figure Xavier meets for the first time when he passes near the Tour de la Frayeur. "He found there a man simply dressed, resting against a tree and absorbed in a deep meditation." Moved by the leper's resignation, Xavier acknowledges that his residence is appropriate for solitude. "What a charming spot! How well designed it is for the meditations of a recluse!" In reply Xavier is informed that the leper's misfortunes are not the result of a frustrated romance, but the product of the humdrum existence of lowly people with more than their share of hard luck. "I lost my parents in my childhood and I never knew them; the one sister I had left has been dead for two years. I never had any friend."[13]

Since mystery frequently enshrouds the origins of an *homme fatal*, the leper complies with the formula. The details of his background, unlike those of the usual colorful Romantic hero, are totally devoid of picturesque elements: "Ah! My name is terrible! I am called *the Leper!* No one in the world knows my family name

and the one given to me by the church on the day of my birth. I am
the Leper; that is the only title I owe to the goodness of men. May
they never know who I am!"[14]

On the theme of love, the leper understands this concept only in
supernatural terms. Earthly love at this juncture in life has no
meaning for him. The literary work that instructs him in the ways of
divine love is the *Imitation of Christ.* To him it is not a book whose
contents must be updated to conform to the humanized theology of
Romanticism and the demands of carnal love. Taking the counsels
of the *Imitation* at face value, the leper accepts them with the zeal
of a medieval cenobite: *"The one who cherishes his cell will find
peace there.* The *Imitation of Christ* teaches us that. I am beginning
to experience the truth of those consoling words. The feeling of
solitude is also mitigated by work. The man who works is never
completely unhappy, and I am the proof of it."[15]

Lamartine also treasured the *Imitation of Christ.* His reading of
this standard and revered work on the spiritual life was slanted to fit
his own needs, a justification of a plaintive and self-centered
melancholy that permeated his poems. Although toward the end
Lamartine adopted an outlook based more on a Christian acceptance of God's will, he never approached the austere example
proposed by Xavier.

Even in a model of resignation there are signs of human frailty.
The inherent modesty of the leper compels him to confess his shortcomings: "I will not deceive you by letting you believe I am always
resigned to my fate; I have not attained this self-abnegation which
some anchorites have achieved. This complete sacrifice of all the
human affections is still not accomplished; my life passes in continual struggles, and the powerful aids of religion itself are not
capable of repressing the impulses of my imagination. . . ."[16]

The existence of the leper has been stripped of any consolations
usually expected in the vale of tears. No one is providing a much-
needed companionship at the time of Xavier's visit. Only one person temporarily lightened the recluse's burden, and now she is
gone. The officer is unable to conceal his sympathy and amazement
at this degree of deprivation. "What! Except for this sister you told
me about, you never had any association, you never have been
cherished by your fellow beings?"[17]

The portrayal of the leper as an orthodox model of the *homme
fatal* is accomplished by Xavier by employing the terminology of
Romantic conventions. Taken out of context, isolated complaints by

the leper could easily pass for the tearful laments of a heartbroken lover. The death of his sister gives rise to an outburst in the best Romantic tradition: "I was for a long time in a kind of stupor which deprived me of the faculty of feeling the extent of my misfortune. When I finally recovered and was in a position to judge my situation, my reason was ready to abandon me. This period will always be doubly sad for me; it recalls to me the greatest of my sorrows, and the crime that almost was the result of it."[18]

Even at the risk of losing Xavier's respect, the leper admits to contemplating suicide. "Already in some fits of melancholy the idea of leaving this life voluntarily had occurred to me; however, the fear of God had always made me reject it."[19]

The death of his dog at the hands of a bestial mob coupled with the sight of two happy lovers strolling in the woods is more than the leper can bear. Any *homme fatal* in a standard Romantic melodrama could not have reacted with a more intense feeling of despair: ". . . I finally conceived the resolution to burn my abode and to permit myself to be consumed with everything that might have left some memory of me. Agitated, furious, I went out into the countryside, I wandered about for some time in the shadows around my residence; involuntary cries came from my afflicted bosom, and frightened me in the silence of the night. . . ."[20]

Despondency yields to the message of hope read in a letter written by his sister just before her death. Instead of the sensation of self-gratification felt by the conventional *homme fatal* on the verge of committing suicide, the leper humbly recites an act of contrition and asks God forgiveness for the rash step he was about to take. What follows is not the vision of a sweetheart with whom the *homme fatal* is reunited in heaven at the foot of the Cross. The leper undergoes a form of mystical experience; his soul momentarily abandons the body to ascend to a higher sphere:

> . . . I saw a cloud spreading over me and I lost the memory of my woes and the feeling of my existence. When I recovered, night had come. As my ideas crystallized, I experienced a feeling of indefinable peace. Everything that had transpired in the evening seemed a dream to me. My first impulse was to raise my eyes to heaven to thank it for having preserved me from the greatest of misfortunes. . . .[21]

Concrete imagery is kept at a minimum in describing the leper's mystical vision—an interlude to assuage the stress imposed by

temptation and to prepare him for a more tranquil phase in his life.
From the ascetic standpoint he has much ground to cover before being able to indulge in calm contemplation of the divinity. The leper
has just avoided perpetrating a sin of despair, which in Catholic
theology is unpardonable inasmuch as the sinner cuts himself off
from God permanently. By the strict standards of the Church's
moral teaching, the leper must pass through a period of atonement.
Once the weaknesses of the flesh are under control and the senses in
submission, the leper will be able to enter into a more intimate
relationship with God. Then the Christian *homme fatal* will be
fulfilled.

Regardless of readers' personal agreement or disagreement with
Xavier's basic premises in *Le Lépreux*, he has, granting these
premises, logically presented a believable version of a Christian
homme fatal. The polemical bitterness associated with Joseph de
Maistre is absent, for Xavier endeavors to get his point across by example. The leper is not a religious fanatic, a zealot determined to
achieve a goal in a manner beyond rhyme or reason; he is an unfortunate human being with all the normal impulses and frustrations.
When he is finally reconciled to his lot, it is traceable to a very
human motivation, a letter of encouragement from a beloved sister.
After passing through many of the stages common to the *homme
fatal*, the leper reaches a solution more compatible with the
precepts of Christianity than the usual decision of the standard
homme fatal in Romantic literature. The latter crushed by calamity
would take a path to self-destruction, a pagan course Xavier cannot
abide. His *homme fatal*, the leper, rejects a meaningless annihila-
tion and chooses a path leading to a sublimation of the baser drives
and a transcendent ideal.

CHAPTER 5

Les Prisonniers du Caucase

I *Background and Summary*

THE original edition of *Les Prisonniers du Caucase* appeared without the author's name in 1815. It was published in Paris by Dondey-Dupré, and printed in the same edition with *La Jeune Sibérienne*. The tale was based on an actual incident that occurred during a Russian campaign in the Caucasus. One of the fierce Caucasian tribes, the Chechens, captured a Russian officer and held him for ransom. Xavier had served with czarist forces in Georgia and was well acquainted with the region. The tale concerns a major, Kascambo, and his orderly, Ivan, and their experiences in captivity among the Chechens. Ivan emerges as the central figure through his ingenuity in planning a successful escape, carried out with startling cunning and bloodcurdling ruthlessness.

II *Reminiscences of Other Writers*

The opening sequence of the *Prisonniers* with the battle between the Cossacks and Chechens resembles any one of several scenes in Balzac's *Les Chouans*. Parallels immediately suggest themselves in even a casual comparison. Russian troops, like the French in *Les Chouans*, are trapped by natives, unerring sharpshooters with an intimate knowledge of the terrain:

The inhabitants of the Caucasus, although individually very courageous, are incapable of attacking en masse, and are consequently not very dangerous for a troop that holds firm, but they have good weapons and fire very accurately. Their superior number on this occasion made the fight too one-sided. After a rather long fusillade, more than half of the Cossacks were killed or incapacitated; the rest had made for themselves a circular rampart with the dead horses behind which they fired their last cartridges. The

Chechens, who always have Russian deserters with them on their expedition, whom they use as interpreters, had them yell at the Cossacks: "Surrender the major to us or you will be killed to the last man" . . . .[1]

Under very similar circumstances, the Chouans in Balzac's novel ambush the ragged recruits from Paris sent to crush the counterrevolution in the Vendée. The Chouans rely as the Chechens do on an ambuscade and the element of surprise on ground unfamiliar to the invader. Equally as fierce as the Chouans and Chechens, the citizen soldiers of France and the Cossacks are relentless adversaries. The markmanship of the Chechens recalls that of the Chouans with their deadly fowling pieces that proved superior to the rifles of the French troops. Loyal to local leaders or chieftains, and bandits and smugglers by nature, the Chechens and Chouans had much in common.

Not always concentrating on the ferocity of the Chechens, Xavier is not above injecting an occasional humorous note into the tale. Ivan's acceptance of Islamism surprises the Chechens, but his conduct as a Moslem soon gives rise to suspicions:

. . . On the other hand, the good Mohammedans, who had favored him at the moment of his conversion, noticed that when he composed his prayer on the roof of the house according to custom, and as the mullah had expressly recommended to him, to win for himself public confidence, he often mixed habitually and inadvertently signs of the cross with prostrations he made in the direction of Mecca, to which he happened at times to turn his back, which made the sincerity of his conversion suspect to them.[2]

Voltaire could not have imparted a more clever twist to the brief description of religious practices that starts in an austere tone and ends in a few words designed to elicit a chuckle from the reader. Xavier most likely was acquainted with *Zadig*, and the *Voyage* previously furnished ample evidence of a finely developed sense of irony and wit.

Insights developed by Xavier and adapted to his writing more than once gave evidence of surprising foresight and an uncanny ability to almost intuit future trends in literature. Thousands of miles away from America, Xavier had no contact with or knowledge of James Fenimore Cooper. Yet in the *Prisonniers* more than one scene furnishes a noticeable parallel with the *Last of the Mohicans* and other novels by the American writer on the Indian. Kascambo's orderly has the astuteness of Natty Bumpo in adjusting to the frozen wastes following the escape from the Chechens, whose similarity to a hostile tribe of Indians can be surmised without difficulty: " . . . Ivan cut pine branches to make a thick bed on the snow on which the major reclined. While he rested, Ivan tried to get his bearings. The valley on whose summit he happened to be was surrounded by high mountains through which no pass could be seen; he saw it was impossible to avoid the beaten path, and that it was necessary to follow the course of the stream to get out of this labyrinth. . . ."[3]

Along with other fugitives from Chechens, Indians, or primitive tribes in general, Ivan and Kascambo have to fend for themselves and be pitiless in seizing upon any means to facilitate their flight. A hapless Chechen youth on a horse is ambushed by them much as Cooper's characters would do in the same circumstances:

> . . . The young man wanted to resist, but seeing the major appear on the bank of the river pistol in hand, he fled as fast as his legs could carry him. The horse was without a saddle, with a halter stuck in the mouth for a bridle. The two fugitives made use of their prize right away to cross the river. This encounter was a stroke of fortune for them for they soon saw that it would have been impossible for them to cross on foot as they had planned. . . .[4]

No scout eluding hostile redmen could have been more resourceful than Ivan. As a woodsman the doughty orderly would have been a reliable partner for Natty Bumpo. Having progressed to the point of exhaustion in their flight through the Caucasian wilderness Ivan, like a character in a Cooper novel, realizes that help from fellow humans is absolutely necessary and sizes up the situation accordingly: " . . . By estimating the distance they had already covered, they judged that dwellings of peaceful Chechens could not be very far away, but nothing was less certain than handing one's self over to these men, whose probable treachery could ruin them. However, in view of Kascambo's weakness, it was very unlikely he could reach Tereck without help. Their provisions were exhausted. . . ."[5]

Without question the general lines of the *Prisonniers* bear an overall resemblance to a typical novel by Cooper on the American Indian. Individual incidents in Xavier's tale constitute in substance key episodes in the novelistic structure developed by Cooper. The flight in the wilderness from primitive tribes, details about living off the land, turning the tables on savages to seize their equipment or steeds to facilitate escape, and the final necessity of seeking help from friendly tribes are standard ingredients in the type of adventure novel evolved by the American writer. It is to Xavier's credit that in a short tale he hit upon a formula that was subsequently put to wide use in Europe and America in the nineteenth century. This is not to say that Xavier alone officially initiated a new trend—far from that. Rather, it is fascinating that Xavier, to whom writing was an occasional occupation, had the insight to choose the Chechens and the setting in the Caucasus to relate in a pleasing style, with an adroit use of techniques and incidents, a story that could serve as a model for future writers. Polygenesis, a derivation from several sources, must be considered as a factor. From this standpoint Xavier would be one of a group of writers who helped establish the general directions of the short story and novel in European and American literature.

III   *Elements of Realism*

Realism, like other terms employed to describe literary movements, can be used arbitrarily unless defined and limited in its application. It may be safely said that the Realistic writer tries to represent the facts as they are, usually does not choose beautiful or harmonious subjects, and depicts instead the ugly and unsavory. Of course, Realism is far more complicated than that when fully considered in all its ramifications. The preceding points, nevertheless, do serve to narrow down the sense in which the term may be used to denote salient features of Xavier's technique in the *Prisonniers*. Students should bear in mind that French critics have regularly used terms such as Classicism, Romanticism, Realism, and Naturalism to describe not only literary movements, but distinctive traits in a writer's style and approach. Thus a critic may speak of the Classical aspects of a Romantic poet or the Romanticism inherent in a Realistic novelist. The need to define terms and restrict their usage does not mean that they can be disregarded. Students with an inclination to dismiss literary history and movements as being of little or no consequence will be at a loss to understand the comments of French critics on their own literature, especially if they read the nineteenth century commentators. The Realism in the *Prisonniers* by Xavier de Maistre has been designated just that. Any arbitrariness exists on the part of those who would reject the term.

The subject selected by Xavier does not present at first sight material suggesting harmony and tranquility. With a scrupulous regard to detail he outlines point by point the procedure followed by the barbaric Chechens in escaping the Cossacks after kidnapping Kascambo and Ivan. Unconcernedly Xavier relates what happens with the detachment of an impartial eye witness:

> After a few hours' halt, the horde proceeded to set out again, when one of their people who had just joined them announced that the Russians were continuing to advance, and probably troops from other forts would gather to pursue them. The chiefs held counsel; it was a matter of concealing their retreat, not only to guard their prisoners, but to keep the enemy from their villages, and thus to avoid his reprisals. The horde scattered along several routes. . . .[6]

The restraint with which Xavier recounts the Chechens' ruses and stratagems does not hide the cruelty that inspires their wiliness. Kascambo and Ivan are prodded along in the manner cattlemen ride herd on recalcitrant longhorns. The author provides the essential information without needless embellishment. Readers have no difficulty picturing the hardships endured by the captives: " . . . The major was so exhausted, that in order to bring him to the stream it was necessary to support him with cinctures. His feet were bloody; they decided to give him back his boots so that he could finish the rest of the trip."[7]

Compassion is foreign to the Chechens, and the major's bloody feet concern them only in terms of rubles and kopecks. No ransom can be expected from the return of a dead hostage and the captors react like merchants afraid of losing precious merchandise: "Kascambo, even sicker from sadness than fatigue, seemed to his guards so weak and distraught that they feared for his life and treated him more humanely."[8] Any show of kindness had a price tag on it. The Chechens, resolved to realize a profit on the officer, take every conceivable step to accomplish their objective. Xavier does not waste words to illustrate the barbaric determination of the Caucasian tribesman. Kascambo is suddenly accorded harsh treatment for a definite reason. Less than a page is required to depict the extent of their inhumanity in extracting from Kascambo a letter to the Russians demanding a large ransom for his release:

> . . . They deprived him of food, they took from him the pad on which he slept and a cushion from a cossack saddle that he used as a pillow, and when finally the go-between returned, he confidently announced to him, that if the demanded sum was refused bluntly, and payment was delayed,

the Chechens were determined to dispose of him to spare themselves the
expense and worry he caused them. The purpose of their cruel conduct was
to induce him to write with a greater sense of urgency. They finally gave
him paper with a reed sharpened in Tartar fashion; they took off the irons
binding his hands and neck so that he could write freely. . . .[9]

In captivity time passes slowly for the major. Only a terse comment from Xavier suffices to maintain the atmosphere of constant
pressure suffered by the browbeaten officer: "Kascambo had
written three letters since his detention without receiving any reply;
a year had gone by. The unhappy prisoner, lacking linen and all the
niceties of life, saw his health decline, and slumped into despair.
Ivan himself had been sick for some time. . . ."[10]

Escape comes at last, but is not pictured by Xavier with a Romantic flourish. Scarcely have the major and orderly left the village
before the precise nature of the arduous trek they must make
becomes apparent to them. Travel without proper clothing, food,
and equipment in the Caucasus in the dead of winter is no pleasure
jaunt, and Xavier has only to supply a few facts to convey the correct impression of the fugitives' plight: " . . . It was in the month
of February; the terrain in these heights and especially in the forest
was still covered with a thick snow that supported the travelers during the night and a part of the morning, but toward noon, when it
had been softened by the sun, they sank down at each step, which
slowed their progress greatly. . . ."[11]

All of Ivan's skill and craftiness cannot offset the physical
obstacles they encounter. At every turn Xavier indicates detail by
detail facts concerning the weather, the forest, the trail, and the
scarcity of food to impress upon the reader the excruciating circumstances of the Russians' flight. The progression observed by
Xavier conveys vividly the increasing hardships experienced by Ivan
and the debilitated major. Having witnessed retreats under wartime
conditions, Xavier was painfully familiar with the suffering un-
dergone by the wounded barely able to walk, a situation now faced
by Kascambo:

> . . . In spite of this favorable rest when he wished to resume his route,
his swollen feet had stiffened to the point that he could not make the
slightest movement without feeling unbearable pain. However, he had to
set out. Leaning on his servant he made his way sadly, convinced that he
would not reach the desired destination. The movement and the warmth
from walking little by little alleviated the pain he felt. He walked all night,

stopping often and resuming his route right away. Sometimes also, giving in to discouragement, he threw himself on the ground and urged Ivan to abandon him to his evil fate. . . .[12]

Less gifted writers would have blown the picture of the major's sufferings out of proportion, but Xavier wisely records one incident and then passes on to another. No amplification is necessary since the facts speak for themselves. Little imagination is required on the reader's part to picture the number of times Kascambo faltered despondently along the way. The terrain to be covered offers more than one pitfall to unwary travelers, and even the alert Ivan cannot anticipate every eventuality. Traversing a frozen stream always presents hazards:

. . . As they were crossing a little ravine on a layer of snow that covered the bottom, the ice broke under their feet and they went into the water up to their knees. Efforts made by Kascambo to extricate himself ended by soaking his clothes. Since their departure the cold had never been so penetrating; the whole countryside was white with hail. After a quarter hour's walk, seized with cold, he fell from fatigue and pain, and refused stubbornly to go further. . . .[13]

If Xavier describes similar incidents, he does so only to emphasize an element essential to the structure of the tale, in this case the prolonged agony of Kascambo. The pace of the narrative never slackens because of time-consuming and irrelevant word portraits. Situations and conditions are depicted as the occasion requires. Once at the end of their strength and resources, Ivan seeks help. There is no fortuitous arrival of a relief column. To the last exasperating moment the orderly has to rely on his native cunning and guile. A neutral Chechen is inclined to offer assistance at a price. Precious minutes must be spent haggling over a settlement while the injured Kascombo is agonizing nearby:

. . . "What assurance will you give me," asked the Chechen, "for the fulfillment of your promise?"—"I will leave you the major himself," replied Ivan. "Do you think I would have suffered for fifteen months, and that I would have brought my master to your place to abandon him here?"—"All right, I believe you, but two hundred rubles are not enough. I want four hundred?"—"Why not ask four thousand? That costs nothing, but since I want to keep my word, I offer you two hundred because I know where to get them, and not a kopeck more. Do you want to put me in the position of deceiving you?"[14]

Right down to the bitter end Xavier traces every step in the painful process leading finally to Kascambo's freedom. When Ivan returns with the sum agreed upon, the wary Chechen, seeing Cossacks in the rescue party, fears he has been trapped and threatens to kill the major. Withdrawal of the soldiers is not enough to satisfy the tribesman, whose gun is still pointed at Kascambo. "The suspicious brigand did not allow him to approach. He made him count the rubles one hundred steps from the house and ordered him to leave."[15] When the major gives the Chechen little assurance of good treatment from his valet, the latter flees in terror from the vengeful Ivan. Xavier does not spare any detail in his true-to-life picture of captivity among the Chechens. Nonetheless, he is selective in his use of facts and inserts no elements to disgust genteel readers. There is no mention of cow dung being used as fuel or of the odors emanating from the stable on the first floor of the house where the prisoners are held. Xavier is content with alluding quickly to Chechen uncleanliness simply by indicating that Kascambo went for months without clean linen. Owing to an unswerving adherence to external detail, the overall atmosphere of the tale is so impersonal that readers are only incidentally interested in Kascambo's release. Ivan's own cruelty rivals that of the Chechens in such a way that little sympathy is evoked either for captor or captive.

IV   *Parallels with Mérimée*

Various details, incidents, and devices in the *Prisonniers* parallel material and techniques employed to good effect by Mérimée.[16] The opening lines of Xavier's tale bring to mind similar scenes in the beginning of more than one story of Mérimée. Could anything be more offhanded and casual than the first brief paragraph where Xavier approaches the subject with the unconcerned air of someone writing an article for an encyclopedia? "The mountains of the Caucasus have for a long time been within the empire of Russia without belonging to it. Their ferocious inhabitants, separated by language and diverse interests, form a large number of little groups, who have few political connections with one another, but who are all animated by the same love of independence and plunder."[17]

Mérimée could not have added a more effective and devastating term at the end than "plunder" to accentuate a distinctly negative feature of the Chechen character. A desire for liberty is an asset, but when linked with wholesale robbery the association suffices to present the tribesmen in a bad light. Xavier immediately commences with a determination, shared by Mérimée, to enter into the heart of the narrative and not stand on ceremony. The geographical location is established and a brief reference to the Chechens is made. In less than a page readers are already being told about Kascambo's party traveling in the Caucasus. A similar celerity in narration typifies *Mateo Falcone, Tamango,* and *Colomba,* to mention a few of Mérimée's better known stories. From the standpoint of technique it constitutes a *volte-face* for the discursive author of the *Voyage* and *Expedition.* The warm, relaxing atmosphere of these two tales is replaced by a deadly seriousness on Xavier's part. A story has to be related, and the author's personal feelings in the matter are of little or no consequence. Mérimée in *Colomba* becomes less impersonal for a moment to tease the reader with an invitation to join other refugees in the Corsican maquis. Xavier too has no time for frivolity save an occasional ironic remark.

No sooner has the locale been described than Xavier relates the attack on Kascambo's party. The reader's introduction to the Chechens is short and abrupt, with their strengths and weaknesses succinctly stated: "The inhabitants of the Caucasus,. although individually very courageous, are incapable of attacking en masse, and are consequently not very dangerous for a troop that puts up a good front, but they have fine weapons and shoot very accurately. Their great number on this occasion made the combat too uneven. After a rather long fusillade, more than half of the Cossacks were killed or wounded. . . ."[18]

A brief but insightful sketch of major characters is often masterfully employed by Mérimée, a technique anticipated by Xavier. Kascambo's lack of judgment and common sense impel him to plunge headlong into certain misfortune: " . . . Impatient to return to his post and brave to the point of temerity, he had the imprudence to undertake this trip with the escort of about fifty Cossacks which were at his disposal, and the still greater imprudence of talking about his plan and of bragging about it before carrying it out."[19]

Courage marks the basic impulses of Kascambo, who surrenders to the Chechens willingly to save the soldiers whose lives he risked. Ironically, just after he hands himself over, a relief column arrives. Xavier tempers this pessimistic turn of events with the generosity of Ivan who unhesitatingly joins the major in captivity. "The brave

servant decided right away to share his fate, and traveled toward
the direction in which the Chechens had withdrawn."[20]

As a focal point in the narrative Mérimée will utilize a central
object that is featured in the development of the plot. The ring
given to Orso by Lydia in *Colomba* is a reminder to resist temp-
tations to commit violence. Xavier singles out the major's musical
instrument as the symbol of a subsequently successful attempt to escape. Attention is drawn to the one object whimsically spared by
the Chechens who "distributed at once the booty brought to them;
they left to the major only a guitar returned to him in derision."[21]

Xavier proceeds to furnish a concise word portrait of the Russians'
painful march to the Chechen stronghold. Another physical object,
the major's boots, stresses the caution exercised by the Chechens to
avoid pursuit (here are echos of both Mérimée and Cooper). "They
took off his iron-heeled boots, which could have left a recognizable
imprint on the ground, and obliged him as well as Ivan to walk
barefoot a part of the morning."[22]

A laconic comment is sufficient to convey a rather vivid impression to the reader of the Russians' plight. From one seemingly insignificant detail much is learned about the characters in the drama
and the *mise-en-scène*. No long discourse on the cruelty of the
Chechens is necessary; the mere fact they required Kascambo to
walk without shoes speaks volumes. The profit motive in terms of
the ransom money helps to bring out their greed. Apparent
kindness is short-lived and is superseded by further brutality as the
Chechens seek to break Kascambo's will. Fearful for his life they
handle him less harshly, but their kindness does not last long:

. . . They treated him well during these trips, granting him sufficient
food and necessary rest. But when he had reached the distant village in
which he was to be definitely kept, the Chechens completely changed their
conduct toward him, and made him undergo all sorts of bad treatment.
They put irons on his hands and feet, and a chain on his neck to the end of
which was attached an oaken block. The orderly was treated less harshly;
his irons were lighter and allowed him to perform a few services for his
master.[23]

Besides the feigned indifference to the situation in the manner of
Mérimée, some of the irony of Joseph de Maistre is also present.
What is surprising is the facility with which Xavier adopts a
technique so unlike that employed in the *Expédition* and *Voyage*.

The economy of expression, directness, and appropriate use of terms all indicate a careful process of composition; he displays a craftsmanship that does not suffer by comparison with Mérimée. The persons in whose home Kascambo is to be held prisoner are the subject of a bare sketch still capable of relaying a marked impression of the actual circumstances in which the major found himself:

> The family of this man called Ibrahim was composed of the widow of one of his sons, thirty-five years old, and a young child, seven to eight years old, named Mahmet. His mother was as mean and more capricious than the old guardian. Kascambo had to suffer a good deal; but the caresses and familiarity of the young Mahmet were subsequently a real distraction for him and even a real support in his misfortunes. . . .[24]

Two Moslem names, Ibrahim and Mahmet, denote the religious barrier separating prisoner and jailkeeper. The adult Chechens, father and daughter-in-law, vie for a certificate in harshness. Thus depised religiously and socially, the pathetic Kascambo must seek comfort from a child, the only one in the family to have kind impulses; adult prejudice has not yet contaminated him. Mérimée evolved still further this sort of emphasis on ethnic and cultural peculiarities. The naïve, impulsive sympathy of the child stands out in touching relief to the adult cruelty and the barren rooms of a semicivilized dwelling. Chilina, the little girl in *Colomba,* comes to mind after studying the portrait of the Chechen lad. Romantics took an interest in children, often indulging in sentimentalized depictions of innocence. The Romanticist in Mérimée moved him to include children in his writings, but only as observed in an actual life setting. If the young Chechen is gentle, his is merely the reaction of one child; Fortunato in *Mateo Falcone* is avaricious and traitorous. There is the unavoidable impression that Xavier would also portray two types of children should a particular story line impose such demands.

Selectivity is a key word in the esthetic principles to which Mérimée subscribes. Totally unaware of future developments in the short story and novelette, Xavier structures the *Prisonniers* along the very lines later seen in Mérimée in more intricate and varied patterns. One episode is necessary to provide an adequate insight into the Chechen temperament and value system. Kascambo's emergence as a judge in internecine disputes aptly serves this function. When one Chechen acts as a messenger for a fellow tribesman in taking a sum of money to another village, he loses his horse in an accident. Angrily the messenger keeps the money as compensation for the dead steed, but the other furiously demands an instant return of the cash. The dull routine of village life is broken with the prospect of a comical trial as the major is called upon to judge the arguments which might well result in bloodshed for friends and relatives of the two adversaries who threaten to settle matters by gun and sword. Adroitly the seriocomic situation is summed up and the Russian officer is forced to hold court: "All the people of the village descended tumultuously on his residence to learn more quickly the outcome of this ridiculous trial. Kascambo was taken from his prison and led upon the platform used as a roof for the house."[25]

For once the major is not cowed into submission. Xavier shows that, when in a position of authority, Kascambo is capable of a firm and resolute courage. Having commanded bellicose Cossacks, he finds nothing substantially different in confronting a Chechen mob divided into two armed camps bristling with pistols and daggers. His captivity had taught him that Chechens had little use for legal niceties:

> Despairing of making the defendant listen to reason, the major had him approach, and, to at least put the scoffers on the side of justice, he put the following questions to him: "If, instead of giving you five rubles to take to his creditor, your comrade had only charged you with bearing a greeting, would not your horse have died just the same?"
>
> "—Perhaps," replied the Chechen.
>
> "—And, in this case," added the judge, "what would you have done with the greeting? Would you not have been forced to keep it in payment and be satisfied? I order you, consequently, to return the money and your comrade to give you the greeting."[26]

Thus thwarted, the furious Chechen reluctantly hands over the cash, all the while cursing the Christian dog for his judicial decision. Xavier cannot resist the temptation to add a touch of irony (Mérimée would have done the same), and to indicate an ethnic trait of the Chechens. The author, after relating the defendant's discomfiture, concludes: "This singular confidence denotes the idea these people have of European superiority and the innate sense of justice that exists among the most ferocious men."[27] Along with the sarcasm, Xavier furnishes an anthropological commentary on the legal notions of semicivilized people. Unlike the Rousseauistic ideal of the noble savage, Xavier depicts primitive men as they actually are. Some of the thinking of Joseph de Maistre on false notions about noble savages is present here. Mérimée held similar views about the myth of the innocent primitive.

Satisfied with this confrontation of two concepts of justice, Xavier returns to the main plot: "Kascambo had written three letters since his detention without receiving any answer; a year had gone by."[28] Time in the *Prisonniers* is not the object of the metaphysical speculations that characterized the *Voyage* and *Expédition*. For Xavier the Realist time is little more than an obstacle to human endeavor; its presence is acknowledged and nothing more. With the same disdain for needless abstractions as Mérimée, Xavier proceeds with the main business at hand, the telling of a story. Theological considerations, so important to Xavier in the *Lépreux,* are disregarded in the *Prisonniers*. Ivan's cynical attitude is an established fact and is recognized as such by Xavier without superfluous moralizing. Shamelessly the orderly confesses to the major: "I can no longer obey you and would hide it from you in vain; I have been a Moslem since the day you thought I was sick and they took off my chains."[29] By no means a believer, Mérimée would, with like insouciance, allude to religion when it had a bearing on the narrative. Ivan's indifference accurately reflects his feelings, and Xavier does not propose to insert an artificial remedy for unbelief in the form of a miraculous conversion. Although Ivan may join the major in making the sign of the cross before hacking a path to freedom through the ice, this gesture of faith has no more meaning for him than any outward signs of piety displayed by the vindictive Colomba.

The orderly has greater confidence in human nature than in religion. The former at least can be confirmed empirically. He does not trust the Chechens. Why? "A little boy told him openly that his father wanted to kill him."[30] Just one sentence is all Xavier needs to convey several impressions to the reader: the natural impulses of a child in a real life situation, Chechen treachery, and, by implication, the reasons for Ivan's own subsequent brutal conduct. Elsewhere Xavier points out that Ivan means *Jean le Doux* or John the Gentle. An ironic assignment of names that signify the direct opposite in a person's makeup was a device to be exploited at an early stage by Mérimée. Fortunato in *Mateo Falcone* is most unlucky; the slave ship in *Tamango—L'Espérance*—symbolizes despair, not hope; its captain coincidentally has the same surname as Ivan—Ledoux.

Careful choice in the use of details, names, or particular incidents is a principle applied shrewdly in the *Prisonniers*. Physical objects have an important function throughout the narrative. Loss of the key to Kascambo's chains impedes the major's mobility and slows down the refugees. The superb carabine, belonging to their jailer, is a source of regret to Ivan who forgot to steal it, emphasizing the orderly's innate cupidity and violence. A far more terrrifying symbol of death is the ax with which Ivan will slaughter all those standing in the way of his escape. The pistol, left with the injured Kascambo by the orderly when he sets out to seek help, is a deadly token of the death that awaits the major should Ivan fail to return. Of all the physical objects in the *Prisonniers* to which some significance is attached, none has a more hopeful symbolism than the hut discovered by the Russians when on the verge of collapsing from fatigue: " . . . It was a sort of chalet, a summer dwelling for Chechens that happened to be deserted. In the fugitives' situation, this isolated house was a precious discovery. Ivan proceeded to snap his master out of his thoughts to lead him to the refuge he had just discovered, and, after having placed him there, set out at once in search of food supplies. . . ."[31]

Whereas the house of Colomba's enemies embodied the unforgiving spirit of a Corsican family caught up in a vendetta, the chalet had a positive meaning for the weary fugitives. Shelter from the cold and a much needed respite were available there.

In speaking of central objects in the *Prisonniers*, when associating Xavier's technique with that subsequently utilized by Mérimée, the focal point is unquestionably Ivan's carefully laid plan to escape. Colomba or Tamango could not have been more cunning. The resourceful orderly loses no time in sizing up the situation in the Chechen village. Worming his way into the confidence of his captors, he stops at nothing to attain his objective. If necessary, he will make himself the butt of ridicule: "To win greater trust he had put himself on the level of a buffoon, conceiving each day some new pleasantry to amuse them. Ibrahim especially liked to see him perform the Cossack dance. When some inhabitant of the village came to visit them, they took off Ivan's chains and made him dance, which he always performed graciously, each time adding some ridiculous gesture. . . ."[32]

Suffering in his captivity more than Ivan, Kascambo has less foresight and imagination in perceiving possible means of escape. His musical ability, however, fits into the orderly's scheme: "The major himself was often forced to sing with his servant Russian songs and to play the guitar to amuse this ferocious society. . . . He was unaware then that one day his guitar would contribute to setting him free."[33]

The foretoken, or *présage*, a frequent element in Mérimée's structuring of a tale, is inserted neatly by Xavier with the purpose of sustaining the general atmosphere of suspense. The greater freedom of movement gradually permitted to Ivan to enable him to better entertain the unsuspecting Chechens is an essential factor in Ivan's scheme. Tamango, in Mérimée's tale of the slave trade, also cleverly played the buffoon, gradually obtained greater freedom of movement, and lulled his guards into a false sense of security before striking a blow for liberty.

Eventually Ivan's patience pays off. The jailer is more kindly disposed toward him, especially when Ivan is ill. "The severe Ibrahim, to the great surprise of the major, had however freed this young man from his chains during his sickness, and left him besides at liberty." Prepared to go to any lengths to insure escape, Ivan embraces Islam with typical callousness. "My name is Houessein now. What harm is there? Can I not become a Christian again when I wish and you are free?"[34] The amorality of a Mateo Falcone or the bandits in *Colomba* could not be summed up more succinctly.

Wiliness accomplishes much in planning an escape, but when dealing with tricky and suspicious tribesmen, the tables can be turned. Ivan discovers this to his dismay. Distrustful Chechens order him to join a raiding party against the Russians so that they can kill him without being detected in the midst of combat. The orderly was bound to have a sinking feeling as he rode forth with the tribesmen: "The Chechens' confidence should have given rise to some suspicion in Ivan's mind; it was not natural for men so guileful and so defiant to admit a Russian, their prisoner, into an expedition directed against his compatriots. It was definitely revealed afterward that they had invited him along only with the intention of killing him. . . ."[35]

An element of melodrama is injected when Ivan, in the nick of time, and at the risk of his own life, rescues one of the Chechens, thus demonstrating what should have been irrefutable proof of loyalty to the cause. Mérimée also made limited use of melodramatic incidents, provided they served a purpose in the general scheme of the study and produced a specific impression on the reader without destroying the pervading unity of the narrative.

Xavier already saw the wisdom of this technique and applied it with good results. Unlike many Romantic writers, Xavier did not have the rescue bring about a complete change in the Chechen attitude toward Ivan. Many were still not convinced and with the craftiness of Colomba waited for further and more persuasive evidence of Ivan's trustworthiness. Equally wary, the orderly sensed the suspicion with which others kept a watchful eye on his activities. "The courage he had just shown, his attachment to his master, increased the fears he had inspired in them. They could no longer look upon him as a buffoon incapable of any undertaking as they had done till then."[36]

In *Tamango* and, especially, *Colomba,* folk songs are used as a means of expressing emotions and of communicating. Ivan loses no time in discovering in guitar playing and singing Russian folk songs a way of plotting an escape right under the jailer's nose: ". . . The major took his guitar when he had something important to communicate to Ivan in Ibrahim's presence, and sang while questioning him; the latter answered in the same tone, and his master accompanied him on his guitar. This arrangement not being a novelty, no one ever noticed a ruse that moreover they had the caution to use only rarely."[37]

There are no gimmicks utilized by Xavier to achieve narrative effects, for he detested the theatricality of Romantic pulp writers who shamelessly capitalized on sensationalistic plots and pat endings in a cheap, commercial effort to sell books. Mérimée had a similar disdain for facile solutions to knotty problems in structure that could be solved artistically through painstaking methods. The guard redoubles his vigilance but dozes at intervals. Then the two prisoners sing softly to one another, prefacing each stanza with a statement about their plans at the decisive moment. Ivan thus informs Kascambo: "See this ax, but do not look at it. Tra, la, la, I will cleave this rascal's skull." To which the major replies anxiously: "Useless murder! Tra, la, la. How will I flee with my irons?"[38]

Ivan, a blood brother of Tamango in stealth and trickery, goes into the customary routine of a Cossack dance with inane grimaces and gestures. (The black chieftain caught the slavers off guard with much the same line of buffoonery.) Intermittently Ivan, when he has the chance, moves the ax from one location to another and continues to dance and sing. Coldbloodedly the orderly suddenly seizes the ax and first kills Ibrahim and then the daughter-in-law who enters the room inadvertently. With the grim brutality of Mateo

Falcone, Ivan shrugs off the major's protests and prepares to finish off Ibrahim's grandson to make sure no one remains to sound the alarm after they flee: ". . . Frightened by this second murder, which he did not expect, the major, seeing Ivan go toward the child's room, stood in front of him to stop him. 'Where are you going, wretch?' he said to him. 'Would you have the barbarity to kill this child too, who showed so much friendship to me?' . . .'"[39]

Ivan, with only one thought on his mind—escape—brushes aside Kascambo with a sneer. "They will never take you alive; I will kill you, them, and myself before that happens."[40] The orderly's overriding obsession—flight to safety—like Tamango's insatiable yearning for freedom and the implacable Colomba's quest for revenge, provides the central theme for the *Prisonniers* and produces the oneness of effect Mérimée was to achieve so often and so brilliantly.

To Xavier's credit, the pace of the narrative does not slacken. The Russians encounter obstacles in their flight, and at the very end they are obliged to seek help from a neutral Chechen. In keeping with the story's unremitting realism, monetary gain, not compassion, induces the Chechen to help them. Colomba in the final pages of Mérimée's novelette remained consistently cruel in temperament; the closing lines of the *Prisonniers* find Ivan unrepentant and as defiant of normal canons of ethics as ever. The person, indicated by the author as the source of the story, tells how he was present at Kascambo's wedding feast where he met Ivan. The latter, on being asked whether he was invited, frightened the inquisitive gentleman out of his wits by recapitulating the song associated with the ax murders: ". . . Ivan gave him a sideward glance, and went into the house whistling the tune *Hai luli*. He appeared soon afterward in the ballroom, and the curious person got back into his sleigh, delighted at not having received a blow in the head with an ax."[41]

Long before the Naturalists, Xavier stumbled upon the bleeding slice of life and capitalized on it with a chilling impersonalism that readers of the *Voyage* would not be apt to associate with the charming and whimsical narrator of room journeys.

CHAPTER 6

La Jeune Sibérienne

I Introduction and Background

*L*a Jeune Sibérienne was published, together with the *Prison-niers du Caucase*, in 1815 in Paris by Dondey-Dupré. The story of a young girl who journeyed to Saint Petersburg in 1801 to seek pardon for her parents was well known in Russia and in France in the early 1800s. A popular French novelist, Mme Sophie Cottin, used the incident as the subject of a novel in 1806: *Elisabeth, ou les Exilés de Sibérie*. This version by Mme Cottin of the valiant daughter who obtained the release of her father from the czar himself, although overshadowed later by Xavier's book, at the time took its place as a best seller with Mme de Stael's *Corinne and Delphine* and Chateaubriand's *Atala*.

Much of the background of *La Jeune Sibérienne* would necessarily be available to Xavier. Unlike other French writers, he had the advantage of a long residence in Russia. Not having been to Siberia personally, he was still in a position to conduct interviews with individuals who either knew the girl or were acquainted with Tobolsk, the village in which the action takes place. The air of authenticity and realism in *La Jeune Sibérienne* indicates a firsthand knowledge and contact on Xavier's part. Lopouloff was the actual name of the girl and her family.

II Social Conditions

Typical of many monarchists, Xavier was essentially kind-hearted and not inclined to favor undue exploitation of the masses. Paternalism to his way of thinking produced the greatest benefits for the common man free from the chaos of unbridled democracy which replaced benevolent despotism with a vicious proletarian tyranny. Under the latter system men unfit to govern usurped the rights of those divinely ordained to rule. Xavier accepts unquestioningly the precepts of his older brother on the subject of monarchy. Autocratic thinking did not keep Xavier from sympathizing with the plight of Prascovie and her family. He is quick to recognize the fraternal bond that unites poor people suffering the same injustices. Two elderly outcasts in Siberia who are close friends of the family exemplify this warm and spontaneous relationship: ". . . The two poor exiles also wanted to contribute to the little sum she was taking along for the trip; one offered thirty copper kopecks and the other a silver piece of twenty kopecks. It was their subsistence for several days. Prascovie refused their generous offer but was deeply moved. . . ."[1]

During her travels Prascovie was exposed to many perils. She has barely begun her journey when along with other young girls she is harassed by intoxicated youths out to gratify their own desires. To get rid of them Prascovie must take some liberties with her normally strict ethical code. Fibbing, she tells the boisterous young drunks that soon brothers will come to meet their sisters and see them safely home. Prascovie senses little remorse in relating a petty falsehood. "It was a little lie," she used to say in telling of her first adventure, "but it brought me no unhappiness."[2] While bent on relating the story of a pious girl, Xavier had no intention of ascribing to her the worst features of a cloying prissiness. Like many human beings, Prascovie will respond to any threats with a normal impulse to defend herself.

Fellow Russians alternately display kindness and cold indifference. Exhausted after spending a rainy night outdoors, she stumbles along the road but not for long. "Happily a peasant who was passing by had pity on her and offered her a seat in his wagon." He lets her off in the next village where luck for the moment goes against her. "The townswoman, after examining her a few seconds with an air of scorn, harshly sent her away." For the devout individual in a Christian country there is always the hope of finding solace at a place of worship. "The young girl, seeing a church ahead of her, went there sadly." However, the doors are locked and she must be content with praying on the steps. Under more favorable circumstances even her father's former military rank works to her benefit—"she was designated a captain's daughter"—and she could take a more positive view of the situation. "She acknowledged nonetheless that the misfortune of being rejected rarely happened to her, whereas the manifestations of human warmth and kindess were innumerable."[3]

This optimism is more than amply justified later when Prascovie, on the verge of expiring from cold and hunger, becomes the object of tender attention and sympathy of poor people traveling with her and sharing the same hardships: "The peasants noticed she had a frozen cheek and rubbed it for her with snow, taking the greatest care with her; but they absolutely refused to take her further, and explained to her that she ran the greatest danger by exposing herself to the cold without a fur garment." The camaraderie among the common people of Russia is vividly demonstrated as Xavier describes how they all eventually decide to take turns going for a while without a fur cloak in order that Prascovie may be warmly dressed. The decision is reached with the spirit of players cooperating in an athletic event. "The girl traveler was placed on a sleigh, wrapped up in a fur. The young man, who had given it to her, covered himself with a mat she had been using till then, began to sing at the top of his lungs, and started them on their way."[4]

The effect of prevailing social conditions on Pascovie manifests itself during a period of recuperation from the hardships of winter travel at the home of some kind ladies. To pass the time profitably she learns how to read and write without ever blaming her family for any deficiency in her education: ". . . This circumstance of her life might give a very bad idea of her parents, for having neglected to this extent the training of their only child, if the thought of an eternal exile had perhaps not caused them to view as useless, or even dangerous, any instruction for their daughter apparently destined to live in the lowest rungs of society."[5] Inequality of opportunity is accepted without protest by Prascovie, who is thankful for the few blessings she receives. The frigid indifference of metropolitan life may make her appreciative of the warm relations experienced back in the small Siberian village. Certainly the urban problems she witnesses at Saint Petersburg cause her to forget momentarily her own difficulties in obtaining a hearing from the authorities. With a mixture of concern and impersonalism, Xavier comments on what are already the bad results of overpopulation and crowding in a confined area: "Such is the makeup of society in a big city: misery and opulence, happiness and misfortune cross paths incessantly, and meet without seeing one another; they are two separate worlds that have no analogy, but between which a small number of compassionate souls establish rare points of contact."[6]

The depth of Xavier's powers of observation are aptly displayed.

Seemingly casual in his perception of the world about him, Xavier upon closer inspection reveals an eye quick to catch in a flash little details of everyday life. Habits acquired as a painter, continued to serve him in good stead in his writing career. The theme of urban suffering, previously noted in the *Voyage*, still haunted Xavier. He must have had difficulty at times reconciling his espousal of absolute rule with his concern about social inequities. His acceptance brings to mind the passivity into which Baudelaire lapsed after being confronted with the insensitivity of the bourgeois. Both writers chose the passive role of the artist refusing to become embroiled in social change. Neither had the stamina of a Hugo or Lamartine in seeking public office as a means of effecting reforms.

Prascovie, on being ushered into the sophisticated ambiance of her benefactor's drawing room, does not feel ill at ease or resentful in the manner of a Rousseau. Instead her ingenuousness gives rise to honest sentiments of amazement and wonder: ". . . On entering the salon she was intimidated by the air of ceremony and the silence that reigned there. The gathering was large in number and divided into groups; the young people were playing around a table in one corner of the room, and all eyes were fixed on her . . ."[7]

Inadvertently a humorous note is introduced into the narrative during the course of a game of boston which the old princess and her friends are playing. After reading a letter, Prascovie has given her, she is slow in resuming the game and an impatient partner reminds the venerable lady a bit sharply: ". . . When he saw the princess fold up the letter, he said in a formidable tone of voice: 'Boston!' Prascovie, already disconcerted, seeing that he was glaring at her, thought he was addressing her, and answered: 'I beg your pardon, sir?' which made everyone laugh. . . ."[8]

Oblivious to the artificiality of a snobbish society, Prascovie with a disarming lack of affectation goes quietly about her business and at last has her request granted by the czar. This of course creates quite a stir in the salon of the princess, although Prascovie is not aware of the changeable whims and caprices of drawing room habitués. Her consistently optimistic slant on human nature enables her to maintain her composure in the most sophisticated gathering:

. . . When she returned at about nine o'clock in the evening she was immediately, and for the first time, called to the salon; the success she had just obtained had effected a small revolution in the mind of everyone. Her good fortune gave the greatest pleasure to her friends and seemed to give even more to persons who, until then, had shown only indifference to her. They noticed she had a pretty figure and beautiful eyes. . . .[9]

Social approval means nothing to Prascovie, totally unconcerned about making an impression calculated to please snobs. Whereas a sensitive artist like Rousseau would react violently to genteel boors, the straightforward Prascovie is so much a stranger to such attitudes that she completely overlooks hypocrisy and pretentiousness. Her own system of values is too basic and honest and is the source of strength that sees her through:

> When she related the details of her story and revealed without thinking the qualities of her noble character, she was never animated by the enthusiasm she inspired in her listeners. She spoke only to satisfy the requests made of her. Her answers were always dictated by a sense of obedience, never by the desire to be brilliant or even interest anyone. Praises lavished on her aroused her amazement, and when they were excessive or even in bad taste, her dissatisfaction became apparent.[10]

Through this brief and pointed commentary on Prascovie, Xavier adds the final dimension to his perception of society in *La Jeune Sibérienne*. The peasant girl has discovered the most genuine manifestation of concern and kindness among the common people. With few exceptions, they have accepted her at face value without questioning her motivations and personality. In general more sophisticated and prosperous members of Russian society acclaim her only after she has achieved some recognition by the royal establishment. A small number of the upper classes demonstrate great kindness and interest, but the greater majority are incapable of appreciating Prascovie's true worth. What Xavier presents is his own individual interpretation of the simple unaffected child of nature contrasted with an ostentatious and brittle society. The subsequent interaction has no traumatic consequences. Her values and those of the habitués of the salon remain unaffected by the mutual exposure. Xavier ostensibly intends to inform readers that the devout, humble person operating on a religious level, accessible to only a few select spirits, is impervious to the blandishments of materialism. This would appear to be his solution to the social dilemma. Admittedly the Romantic era spawned revolutions throughout Europe, but Xavier considers this an inadequate response to the challenge of the times. Since monarchy for him is a direct reflection of the divine will, then the solution for the individual overcome by the inevitable hardships of life must be resignation to that will. The author does not counsel passivity, for Prascovie acts on her convictions; but she does so within the existing social framework.

If Romanticism in the final analysis is the spirit of individualism manifested in diverse forms then Xavier certainly provides his own unique version of and approach to the quandary of Romantic man.

III *Romantic Elements*

Romantic traits in *La Jeune Sibérienne* are in no sense wild and impulsive in their manifestation for Xavier exercises considerable restraint. The strict Classical side of his esthetic views is noticeable in Prascovie's remarks on the paintings on display at a museum where she was especially pleased by subjects taken from scripture. These she recognized immediately. Prascovie was less impressed when viewing a portrait on a pagan theme:

. . . But passing before a large painting by Luca Giordano, which represents Silenus intoxicated, supported by revelers and satyrs, she exclaimed: "There is a bad picture! What does it represent?" They told her the subject was taken from the fable. She asked from what fable. As she had no idea of mythology it would have been difficult to give her a satisfactory explanation. "Is all that true?" she asked. "There are men with goat's feet. What madness to paint things that have never existed, as though there were not enough authentic ones!" . . .[11]

Prascovie's reaction, as related by Xavier, approximates that of the hidebound Classicist who deemed Homer too extreme by reason of vulgar incidents and emotions depicted in his epics. Serenity and harmony associated with many biblical motifs were more to her liking. Anything grotesque on the order of a satyr did not conform to her notion of verisimilitude. Illogical flights of the imagination had no place in her limited but severe code of esthetics. Such thinking is a reflection of Xavier's opinion on truth in art. Even in a fanciful essay treating armchair travel he stayed within bounds cultivated Frenchmen would judge reasonable and proper.

Restrained by a Classical temperament in the use of Romantic themes, Xavier proceeds with circumspection in *La Jeune Sibérienne*. The story itself of a pious Christian girl did not comply with the strictest canons of Classicism which feared the risk of blasphemy in any literary treatment of Christianity. Placing the locale in Russia of course automatically classified it as an exotic subject, a feature not entirely acceptable to Classical theorists but welcomed, on the other hand, with enthusiasm by Romantics. Prascovie herself has a certain air of mystery about her, not being cut out for pioneer life in Siberia. "Her delicate hands seem to have been formed for other occupations."[12] The father also, a highstrung individual, dreams often of a happier existence elsewhere, and is occasionally surprised by Prascovie in the act of shedding tears. Melancholy pervades the household as the father laments frequently the cruel fate that deprived him of his military career and sentenced him to a harsh exile.

The most Romantic aspect of *La Jeune Sibérienne* is Prascovie's search for a religious ideal, not entirely satisfied by the quest for justice on her parents' part and finally realized by her entry into the convent. Some influence of the Romantic stage is discernible in isolated episodes; in one of these she follows her father into the garden to beg him to consent to a trip to Saint Petersburg to seek a pardon from the czar:

. . . "Believe it is the will of God. Do you want to force your daughter into the terrible unhappiness of disobeying you?" Speaking thus, Prascovie embraced his knees and tried to inspire in him the same confidence that animated her. The mother arrived. Her daughter implored her to be of assistance in making the father give in. . . . Lopouloff, however, could not resist any longer such touching entreaties. . . .[13]

Her departure from the homestead takes place in a rather idyllic vein. The father and mother resemble the family heads in many Romantic novels and are one dimensional. They alternately smile and shed copious tears. Much of their time is spent in bemoaning their fate. Aside from providing the necessary atmosphere for the development of the plot, the parents add little to the story. The farewell scene, just the same, is described simply, with little fanfare or adornment:

Prascovie kneeling received the blessing of her parents and, tearing herself courageously from their arms, left forever the hut which had served as a prison to her since childhood. The two exiles accompanied her for the first mile. The father and mother motionless on the threshold watched her for a long time, wishing to bid her a last farewell from a distance; but the girl no longer looked back and soon disappeared in the distance.[14]

Xavier's sense of proportion allows him to permit one melodramatic incident to vary the pace of the tale. He appreciates the value of Romantic techniques for exciting and maintaining readers' interest by heightening the suspense on occasion. Like Mérimée he carefully selects the moment when such an episode can be used effectively. Unlike Romantic hackwriters who accumulated one incident after another with no regard for credibility, Xavier chooses one moment in the course of Prascovie's journey: "Among the distressing situations on her trip there was one in which the girl believed her life threatened and which merits being known for its singularity." Obliged to stop at the home of a surly, suspicious-looking couple, Prascovie is horrified when they ask how much money she has and refuse to believe her purse only contains eighty kopecks. "The girl protested in vain that it was all she had; they did not believe her. The wife sneered with her husband."[15]

Huddled in a corner near the stove that night Prascovie fearfully watches the couple search her belongings; they do not disturb the girl and soon retire. In the morning their attitude has changed for the better; they assure Prascovie they thought at first she was a thief. Nevertheless, the frightened young traveler wastes no time in leaving, grateful she is still alive: "When she had gone a few miles out of the village she had the urge to count her money. The reader will without doubt be as surprised as she was on learning that instead of eighty kopecks that she thought she had, she found a hundred and twenty. Her hosts had added forty."[16]

By limiting himself to one exciting anecdote with the right amount of melodrama, Xavier could please readers with Romantic sensibilities and still observe his own code of esthetics. Another incident in the story is by comparison a bit maudlin and superfluous, although in all probability Xavier honestly thought it served to stress Prascovie's sincerity and trust. The Romantic element is presumably present in the air of mystery with which a kindly, though eccentric, lady hides her identity from Prascovie. She leads the weary young traveler to the home of a Mme Milin and allows the girl to discover the truth for herself: "Prascovie entered the house and, addressing the servants of Mme Milin, asked them if their mistress was home. The domestics, astonished at being asked this question in the presence of their mistress herself, answered nothing. . . . Finally, one of the women said, 'Why there she is!' . . ."[17]

Prascovie of course learns that the lady who guided her to the house is none other than Mme Milin. Xavier at times tends to impart to the narrative a childlike tone reminiscent of a fairytale. What he accomplishes by avoiding excessive melodrama and depicting scenes ostensibly taken from real life is offset now and then by contrived and Pollyannaish situations designed to relieve some temporary distress experienced by Prascovie. This tendency does not get out of hand and Xavier makes up for it by episodes and scenes that are a faithful reflection of life in Russia. One physical symptom is believable, in view of the cold weather, and is also a Romantic convention. Prascovie's respiratory afflictions are justifiable on both accounts: " . . . Since her fall into the Volga, she had a deep cough that bothered her a good deal. A burning fever developed before long; however, although the doctors themselves feared for her life, she was never worried. 'I do not believe,' she said, 'that my hour has come yet, and I hope God will permit me to carry out my project.' "[18]

Much like an opera, where the heroine is slowly dying of consumption, Prascovie gradually succumbs to the pulmonary disorder contracted during the arduous journey to Saint Petersburg. While following in the steps of many a heroine struck down by the dreaded yet fashionable malady of Romanticism, Prascovie's death is rescued from the banality that plagued a large number of her counterparts in Romantic literature. Her demise in the convent does not leave a lonely and sorrowful lover pining for her:

> The nun knelt down again; while she recited prayers, the dying girl from time to time made signs of the cross. The night grew somber.
> When the nuns returned with a light, Prascovie was no longer alive. Her right hand was resting on her chest, and they saw, from the position of her fingers, that she had died making the sign of the cross.[19]

Romantic love assumed various forms and was often mixed with Christian theology to give it a veneer of respectability. Lovers assured themselves that love in any form, even extramarital, was pleasing in the eyes of God whose Son died on the cross through love of mankind. Thus the carnal was sublimated by the divine. Lamartine in "Le Crucifix" exemplifies this version of Romantic love when justifying an adulterous relationship with the thought that his sufferings parallel those of Christ.

Xavier, more consistent in the type of love depicted in *La Jeune*

Sibérienne, has no need to equivocate. Carnal love does not enter into the picture, for Prascovie's fulfillment is realized in another world. Her passions and emotions are refined and dedicated to a higher goal. Regardless of readers' individual theological viewpoints, it must be conceded that Xavier does not stoop to fence straddling. For him the issue is clear-cut. If love is to be interpreted in strictly religious terms, then the lines dividing the material and spiritual orders must be firmly drawn. No true mystical union with God by any Christian definition, he feels, can be achieved in which the recipient of divine love is harboring at the same time a mistress in his chamber.

IV   *Elements of Realism*

From the very beginning of *La Jeune Sibérienne,* Xavier clearly establishes one of his main goals—to follow as accurately as possible the factual details of a young girl's quixotic effort to liberate her parents. He does not intend to burden the story with gory incidents, nor does he wish to lapse into a fanciful yarn and a foolishly Romantic plot with no regard for a logical outcome. Side by side with Romantic elements there are features associated with Realism. In this connection Xavier announces his intention to use a narrative form documentary in tone: "If the account of these adventures does not offer that interest based on surprise that a novelist can inspire for imaginary personages, one will read not perhaps without some pleasure the simple tale of her life, rather interesting in itself, without any adornment other than the truth."[20]

Xavier sticks to the main story line with few digressions and superfluous episodes. Prascovie, a prayerful young landy, leads a normal family life. She is not in any sense an overnice girl incapable of any transgression. On the contrary, her parents can be annoyed with her. A tactless attempt to blurt out to her father a desire to see the czar arouses his ire and laughter in which the mother joins: " 'Let us get busy,' she said handing her a rag, 'start by cleaning the table for supper; you can then leave for Saint Petersburg at your convenience.' "[21] "

Piety had no rewards in the village and, besides being temporarily rejected at home, Prascovie also encounters ridicule among the townspeople. One, in particular, through his derision personifies the forces of irreligion that sneer at the young girl's dream of a successful pilgrimage to Saint Petersburg. Neiler, the tailor, former-

ly a valet to a university student in Moscow, fancies himself a
philosophe. Overlooking his jibes at her earnest faith, Prascovie
seeks his help to obtain a passport. This routine request unmasks the
braggart: "Unfortunately the *philosophe* did not know how to
write; he confessed that since the moment he had dedicated himself
to the tailoring profession he had totally neglected literature."[22]

The pseudorationalism of a Neiler is objectively treated along
with the shortcomings of Christians in the village. Prascovie's
mother is superstitious and is afraid to upset a salt shaker and incur
a streak of bad luck. Scripture itself is submitted to the demands of
superstition not satisfied with revelations in the gospel:

> . . . Sometimes she took the Bible, and opening it haphazardly, she
> sought in the first sentence before her eyes something analogous to her con-
> dition and from which she might draw a good prediction. This manner of
> consulting fate is very much in use in Russia; when the sentence is insignifi-
> cant they start over, and by twisting the meaning a little they end up with
> the desired turn of phrase. . . .[23]

Although himself a practicing Christian, Xavier does not allow his
own convictions to color the facts. He is quite capable of reporting
circumstances without slanting the account to fit his views. When
Russians stoop to superstitious practices in the name of religion he
will not gloss over the details but submits them to the reader's judgment. Mérimée, a freethinker, reacted the same way. Religious
practices as depicted in *Colomba* and *Mateo Falcone* are merely a
commentary on customs common to special ethnic groups. No
Voltairean diatribes are directed at organized religion. Both Xavier
and Mérimée, one a believer and the other an agnostic, discarded
personal beliefs in the interests of objectivity in what was undeniably one positive aspect of a Realistic approach.

Mérimée and Xavier were also equally concerned about the
proper use of local color. Neither employs this device excessively
and both limit it to those points in the narrative where some
elaboration on particular customs is required. Even then it is not
employed as an excuse for a lengthy disgression of several pages,
but invariably is summed up in a pithy paragraph. A case in point is
Prascovie's preparation to depart on her pilgrimage:

> At that moment the last rays of the setting sun shone in the room. "The
> hour has come," she said. "We must separate." She sat down, as her

parents and the two friends did, as it is customary in Russia on such an occasion. When bidding a final farewell, the traveler sits down; all persons
present must imitate her; after a minute's rest, during which they talk
about the weather and indifferent things, they get up and the tears and embraces begin.[24]

Underlying the type of Realism utilized by Xavier is a painstaking
effort to avoid sordid details that would destroy the artistic effect of
the work. Conditions are described in their bare outlines without
enumerating all the unpleasant features of a character's situation.
Much is left to the reader's imagination. On the whole this technique is quite effective. The text remains unencumbered by verbosity
and the rhythm of the narrative is unimpaired. Prascovie's suffering
from the elements necessitates no tedious listing of all the symptoms of frostbite: " . . . She got under a pine surrounded by high
hedges to protect herself from the violence of the wind. The storm
lasted all night; the girl spent it without shelter in this deserted
spot, exposed to the torrents of rain that only stopped toward morning. When the dawn appeared she dragged herself to the road to
continue on her way. . . ."[25]
Another reality to which Prascovie must adjust, and perhaps with
more difficulty than a rainy night in the open, is human nature.
Obliged to rely on the kindness of villagers for food and shelter, she
quickly learns that vagabonds are regarded by many with suspicion.
She is often accused of being a thief and prostitute. Through a
gradual process she becomes better able to dispel doubts about her
intentions. Generous people as well as the habitually distrustful demand proof of her identity and destination:

 . . . They must be moved without suspecting anything, and they give
their pity more willingly than their esteem. Prascovie used to begin by asking for a little bread, then she spoke of the fatigue that overwhelmed her, in
order to obtain hospitality; finally, when she was established at her hosts,
she told her name and related her story. It is thus that on her painful trip,
she experienced little by little the cruel apprenticeship of the human
heart.[26]

The Russian winter is a constant menace to the unwary wayfarer,
and more than once Prascovie owes her life to concerned people
who refuse to allow her to risk death by traveling alone. Forced to
spend long periods in a hamlet until the roads are passable,
Prascovie patiently follows the sound advice of experienced adults:

The season was advancing; Prascovie was held up almost a week in a village by snow, which had fallen in such abundance that roads were impassable for pedestrians. When they were sufficiently packed down by sleds, she courageously got ready to continue her trip on foot, but the peasants where she had lodged dissuaded her and made her see the danger. . . . .[27]

A persistent wind that constantly covered up road tracks with fresh snow was one obstacle to travel. One even more formidable was the icy waters of the rivers that occasionally had to be forded along the route to Saint Petersburg. At any moment travelers could be tossed into a cold stream by the erratic movements of the boat. The girl is the unhappy victim of such an incident: " . . . Three passengers, among them Prascovie, were thrown into the river. They were pulled out right away, and the young girl was not hurt; but the shame she felt at changing her clothes in front of everyone made her allow them to dry on her; a violent cold was the result of this accident, which had a bad effect on her health."[28]

Modesty, ill-advised under the circumstances, has ultimately sad consequences for Prascovie's well-being. Xavier leaves no stone unturned to lend an air of everyday life to the incidents in the girl's slow and torturous trip. Fidelity to her announced purpose and the strict code of conduct to which she adheres prove to be her physical undoing. In large measure Xavier's persistence in using only the necessary details and facts through a selective application of Realistic devices serves to produce the unified effect of *La Jeune Sibérienne*. Much of the Realism in the story is attributable to the inherent Classicism in Xavier's temperament. Reality could not be presented in all its distasteful aspects, but rather had to be restricted and adapted to an artistic mold.

V   *Political Aspects*

All allusions to the political order in Russia are made with due respect to the reigning house. In no way does Xavier hint that existing injustices call for armed revolt. His acquiescence to the czarist regime is that of a dutiful subject recognizing the divine right of kings. Joseph de Maistre could not have asked for a better example of the political philosophy advocated in the *Soirées* and *Considérations*. As a disciplined and factual observer, Xavier does not refrain from mentioning some of the inevitable consequences of absolutism.

The necessity of having a passport in order to leave Siberia to seek a pardon for her parents provides one of the underlying political motifs in the story. Faced with the inflexibility of the Siberian governor, Prascovie soon realizes that her departure is by no means assured: "Another difficulty was encountered and one more real than the opposition of her father; she could only leave with a passport, without which it was not possible for her to withdraw from the village. On the other hand it was scarcely probable that the governor of Tobolsk, who had never answered their letters, would consent to grant them this favor. . . ."[29]

When unexpectedly the passport finally does arrive there is no explanation whatsoever for the governor's reasons. Government officials in *La Jeune Sibérienne* function as demigods condescending from their exalted positions to intervene from time to time in the affairs of hoipoloi. A physical object, the passport, is a mute symbol of the autocratic power hampering what would seem a routine matter, the right to travel about unimpeded by bureaucratic red tape. Yet this did characterize life under the czar: "It was a moment of joy for the family. In the total abandonment in which they had been for so many years, the sending of this passport seemed to them a sort of favor. However there was in the package no answer from the governor to the personal requests from Lopouloff. . . ."[30]

The passport, once obtained, is a key to free passage. Whenever confronted by the demands of officialdom during her trip, Prascovie has only to display the magic document. "The mayor of the village examined her passport and declared it was in order."[31] Overawed by any sign of authority, Prascovie, once at the Russian capital, tries to give her written request to a senator but has a difficult time endeavoring to find one. Too many high and mighty figures are passing to and fro: " . . . She saw several persons getting out of a carriage and going up the stairs; they all had sword, boots, and uniform; some had epaulettes. She thought they were officers and generals, still waiting to see a senator arrive, who, according to the idea she had formed, had to have something special that would cause him to be recognized. . . ."[32]

Persistence is a dominant trait in Prascovie. She has given a mystical interpretation to her quest and anticipates results in the form of miracles or sudden, gratuitous revelations. To this end the czar himself becomes a God figure in her imagination. Her father encourages the formulation of this image when he pictures the inaccessibility of the czar in the imperial palace. God in heaven could not be more aloof to mere mortals: " 'Alas,' her father answered her shedding tears, 'do you think, poor child, that anyone can talk to the emperor as you do to your poor father in Siberia? Sentinels guard on all sides the avenues to his palace, and you will never be able to pass the threshold. Poor and mendicant, without proper dress or recommendations, how will you dare to appear, and who will deign to present you?' "[33]

With this image fixed in her mind by paternal admonition, Prascovie approaches the czar's palace in trepidation. Just as statues in a cathedral remind believers of the divine presence, so does a statue of Peter the Great recall to obedient Russian subjects the religious significance of the nation's political institutions based on a God-given right. A friend points out the statue to Prascovie and warns her not to expect too much from intermediate officials in the regime. There is only one God in heaven and one czar in Russia: " . . . 'In your place I would leave the senate and the senators who will do nothing for you. It is all as though," she added, showing the statue of Peter-the-Great next to her, 'you were to submit your petition to that statue there. You will obtain nothing.' "[34]

The statue serves a politicoreligious function in Prascovie's decision to persist in her mission. When praying to God to intercede with the czar she transfers some of the divine majesty to the temporal grandeur of the emperor. It is as if she must pray to God under two aspects—the supreme authority in heaven and the supreme authority on earth. When thinking in gratitude of God's favors she associates it somehow with the statue of a czar: " . . . When she passed before the senate, she recalled the promise made to God to return there only one more time. 'His goodness,' she thought, 'has accomplished more than I had asked, for I will no longer have to go back there; and this iron man has also rendered me a service through the grace of God,' she said looking at the statue of Peter the Great. . . ."[35]

Pursuing the theme of the emperor as God figure, Xavier imputes a supernal function to the empress as well. Prascovie approaches her in the manner believers in the Roman and Eastern churches sought the intercession of the Blessed Virgin. The young peasant girl addresses Her Majesty with the familiarity and confidence of a devotee of the rosary: "Without making the slightest inquiry about the manner in which she was to present herself, she entered calmly into the empress' chamber. Her majesty received her with her well-known kindness and asked her about the details of her story. . . ."[36]

Never was a prayer answered by God the object of greater gratitude than that experienced by Prascovie after the czar has granted her request. Later, when ushered into the throne room, she looks upon the symbol of imperial power with a reverence normally reserved for Christ:

> . . . She clasped her hands growing pale. . . . Prascovie, kneeling at the foot of the throne, kissed the steps in ecstasy and bathed it in tears. "Oh, my father," she exclaimed, "behold where the power of God has led me. Oh, my God, bless this throne, bless the one who occupies it, and grant that his days be filled with all the happiness with which he has overwhelmed me!"[37]

Other characters in *La Jeune Sibérienne* also come to view the emperor as a God figure. The two outcasts in Siberia, friends of Prascovie and her parents, had abandoned all hope of pardon even when learning the news that the father and mother of the girl have had their request granted. However, upon learning that the pardon extends to them as well they immediately break into a prayer of thanksgiving: "No language can describe such a situation. For a few minutes only disconnected phrases were heard: "Thank you, emperor! May God be blessed! May God be praised! May he overwhelm the good Prascovie with his favors! . . ."[38]

The czar continues to enjoy an important role in the resolution of the story. In the almost theocratic climate in which Xavier has the action transpire, the political aspects can be fully understood only when taking the religious framework of the author's thinking into consideration. Given this particular perception on Xavier's part, any reference to social conditions in *La Jeune Sibérienne* would understandably be made from the standpoint that such are the facts of life in Russia. Peace and tranquility can prevail only through a stable government guided by a ruling class that allows a few benefits to trickle down to the common people. With a bloody upheaval similar to the French Revolution as an alternative, Xavier sees no need to justify his position.

VI *Religious Aspects*

Prascovie's pious and introspective disposition would normally be best suited to a life of seclusion in a convent, but family obligations force her to take an active role in obtaining her father's release. While accepting this duty resolutely and seeing it through with great success, she senses the need of maintaining her inner resources through private conversations with God. The desire to withdraw from people to pray in private manifests itself early in the story:

> She had chosen on the edge of a grove of birch trees near the house a favorite place where she often retired to pray; she was subsequently even more punctilious about going there to pray to God, with all the fervor of her young soul, to favor her trip and give her the strength and means to carry it out. Abandoning herself to this idea, she often forgot herself in the woods, to the point of neglecting her ordinary occupations, which brought reproaches from her parents. . . .[39]

A tendency to overlook immediate reality is common to many mystics bent on transcending the material order to see God face to face. It is Prascovie's good fortune to be able to adjust to the work-a-day world when duty calls, but throughout the story her disinclination to participate fully in mundane affairs is already a foretoken of her eventual decision to take the veil. Like many saints of humble origin, Prascovie has an intuitive understanding of divine truths. A syllogistic approach would be foreign to her nature: "This religious spirit, this lively faith in so young a person, must appear all the more extraordinary, since she did not owe them to education. Without being irreligious, her father cared little about praying, and although her mother was more consistent in this regard, she generally lacked training, and Prascovie was indebted to herself alone for the feelings that animated her. . . ."[40]

An uninformed faith, totally divorced from any complicated system of metaphysics, stands her in good stead when confronted with obstacles discouraging enough for an adult but almost insurmountable to an inexperienced young girl. Luckily, her reliance on the Lord is tempered by a down-to-earth sense of humor. Xavier has no need to go to great lengths to demonstrate this facet of Prascovie's temperament. One incident suffices when she tells off the arrogant Neiler, who ridicules her habit of praying since he, not the Lord, carried her laundry to the river bank: ". . . 'How could I,' she said to him, 'not put all my trust in the goodness of God? I only prayed a second at the edge of the river, and if my wash did not come alone, it at least came without me and carried by an unbeliever. So the miracle took place; I do not ask any other of Providence. . . ."[41]

The author recognizes the importance he assigns to religious motivation in the resolution of the story and is anxious to indicate to readers his awareness of this theological factor in developing Prascovie's characterization. *La Jeune Sibérienne*, if not a tale of the supernatural, is at least an account of an event where otherworldly motives come into play:

> To some persons these details may appear childish and minute, but when they see that the projects of this girl succeed beyond her hopes and all probability, in spite of the obstacles without number she had to surmount, they will be convinced no human motive would have sufficed to lead her to the goal she set for herself, and for such a work it took this *faith that moves mountains.* . . .[42]

There is a cruel symbolism in the challenges posed to Prascovie's faith. In one town a closed chapel personifies the official indifference of her own church, the Russian Orthodox. Only a lay person in that village saves her from spending another night in the snow. It is probably no mere coincidence that nowhere in the story is there any mention of the Orthodox Church, let alone any direct contact on Prascovie's part with the clergy. Xavier may have wished to adopt the general outlines of a tale that could easily take place in a Catholic country. Except for recognition of the Holy See, the Russian Church preserved the Sacraments, the apostolic succession of bishops, and the mass, and had provisions for monastic life. Subsequently Prascovie does join an Orthodox convent of Russian nuns.

A salutary factor in the formation of Prascovie's religious outlook is her common sense. Although in some respects she may appear a bit Rousseauistic in her intuitive approach to religion, she experiences no feelings of dismay when first introduced to more sophisticated forms of worship. Learning to read does not produce any negative reaction. Instead she adapts herself easily to more formalized ways of praying:

> . . . She began to study with all the ardor and strength of her character, and in a month was in a position to understand a book of prayers given her by her protectors; they were often obliged to tear her away from this occupation. The pleasure she experienced in finding in these prayers the natural sentiments of her heart developed and expressed in so clear and touching a manner made her desire instruction eagerly. . . .[43]

Drawing closer to Saint Petersburg, Prascovie passes through more towns and sees churches and convents more frequently. These abundant signs of Christianity cause her to renew a vow to eventually become a nun. On the other hand, in more populous sections of the country she discovers reasons for being disheartened. Prascovie is not quite prepared for the test to her faith presented by urban problems.

> . . . Since society began to be known to her, she perceived obstacles of another kind, against which all her courage could not sustain her. After having escaped the wilderness, she sensed this frightful solitude of the big cities, where the poor man is alone in the midst of the crowd, and where, as though through a horrible spell, he sees about him only eyes that do not look and ears deaf to his pleas.[44]

A pre-Baudelairean theme becomes a part of Prascovie's mystic vision and has a twofold effect on her. She is better able to cope with the situation in Saint Petersburg, after having acquired some idea of the miseries of metropolitan existence. At the same time Prascovie's determination to renounce life in society is strengthened by what she has seen and heard. On passing through the city of Nijeni, she visits an Orthodox convent and decides to join the nuns there once her mission is accomplished. Her reaction to the convent and the joy she feels give a fuller meaning to her quest, a hard pilgrimage with the immediate goal of helping her parents and the ultimate objective of proving herself worthy of the religious life. When asked by the superior about her purpose in this world, Prascovie, somewhat confused, tries to answer: " 'Do I know myself,' she replied, 'what God requires of me? I wish, I sincerely desire, to end my days here; and if such is the will of Providence, who will oppose it?' "[45]

The divine plan unrolls before Prascovie and after not a few hardships she is allowed some comfort in the knowledge that her ideals are shared by others. Xavier in a subtle way alternates good and bad examples of human nature, wishing to provide readers with a balanced picture. Prascovie has some reason for optimism when she meets Mme V—— who will help her obtain an audience with the czar: "When persons of real merit, when good souls meet for the first time, they do not make each other's acquaintance; it can be said they recognize each other as old friends, who were separated only by distance or inequality in social rank."[46]

Xavier, in calling attention to a rigid class system, does not intend to be snobbish but rather to indicate that pious people can transcend these artificial barriers. The above passage has a somewhat scriptural tone that is repeated as the dénouement draws near. Prascovie has the air of a biblical figure as she greets her parents after having obtained the pardon for them: " 'It is God alone who has done that! Let us thank his generosity for the miracle wrought in our favor.' "[47]

The reunion of the Lopouloffs lasts only a short time, for soon afterward she announces her decision to enter the convent. Prascovie's parents, never able to grasp their daughter's motives whether they involve a trip to Saint Petersburg or a desire to become a nun, demonstrate again their inability to think on the same level as Prascovie. The Lopouloffs are too earth-bound to understand the spiritual order envisaged by Prascovie. Her mother especially fails to comprehend: ". . . 'What good,' she said, 'has this so longed for liberty done us? All the work, all the success of our dear daughter were thus designed only to snatch her from our arms forever? Would we were still in Siberia with her!' Such were the unhappy mother's complaints."[48]

In looking about in French history for a model of the religiously inspired course of action taken by Prascovie, the example of Joan of Arc comes to mind. Extolled by the Catholic Church in France as the girl of humble origins elevated to a spectacular role in answering the divine call and saving her country, she has been the subject of glorification and ridicule in secular literature. Shakespeare in *Henry VI* dismissed her as a conniving wench, and Voltaire interpreted Joan in a rather perplexing manner. To Xavier the moment was ripe for a positive view of the Maid of Orleans, and possibly he thought the salient features of her life could be given a newer and fresher meaning by drawing some subtle parallels between Joan of Arc and a simple, devout girl from Siberia. The time was propitious since rationalism was in disrepute in many quarters and believers looked for a more traditional Christian tone in belles-lettres.

Without pressing his point unduly Xavier presents a sufficient number of similarities between Prascovie and Joan to allow readers to draw their own conclusions. Both young women were illiterate and at first the object of ridicule when they announced their intended purpose. Joan's inspiration is openly associated with divine voices directing her. Prascovie is impelled by a religious determination although not based on direct revelation of God's will. In the case of each, parental opposition must be overcome. Joan arrives at the king's palace, recognizes the uncrowned monarch despite attempts to deceive her, leads the French troops to victory, and eventually suffers death. Prascovie's experiences are less spectacular, although hardships of winter travel in Russia approximate somewhat those endured in a military campaign. Like Joan, Prascovie copes successfully with an effeté and sophisticated society. Her health, undermined by tribulations to which she has been subjected, deteriorates inevitably and she dies soon after entering the convent. Whereas Joan's goal is expressed in the active life, Prascovie's objective is ultimately realized in contemplation. This latter ideal is more in keepng with the Romantic motif of solitude and melancholy. Xavier succeeds in giving an orthodox exposition of religious motives without openly propagandizing on behalf of Christianity.

Any interpretation of Prascovie's characterization depends on the extent to which an individual reader may or may not accept the role of the supernatural as a factor in the Siberian girl's course of action. To those generally in agreement with Xavier's position, the question is not complicated. A pious young girl wishes to aid her parents and prays to God for guidance. Eventually her prayers, after excruciating trials, are answered. Kind people aid her along the weary trek to Saint Petersburg where she finds more influential friends to assist in presenting her request to the czar. Her own sincerity of course plays no small part in obtaining her father's release. It is entirely reasonable in view of the outcome that Prascovie would express her gratitude to God and consecrate the rest of her life to his service.

Another reaction on the part of many readers would be to dismiss *La Jeune Sibérienne* as a fetching little fairy tale. There is room, however, for a third interpretation by those eager to examine conscientiously and objectively the *raison d'être* of any pattern of conduct, especially one not in conformity with average norms of behavior. Ideas that are logically possible can produce delusions in some persons causing them to lose all sense of proportion. Making a trip to see the czar is conceivable but not likely for a tender girl in the dead of winter. In a sense Prascovie's fixation tends to be grandiose; her pleas will influence, she is confident, the czar's course of action. To a mild degree Prascovie's impulses have some of the earmarks of obsession; recurrent thoughts intrude upon her consciousness. She also suffers somewhat from compulsiveness and feels the need to repeat certain acts, namely, her prayers and constant requests for parental permission to make the journey. Once on her way she persists in her prayers and periodically repeats her resolution to see the czar. Prascovie is able to objectify her obsessions and compulsions by making the trip and does not sink into despair and listlessness. Luckily for her she can express her feelings positively in a manner that conforms to the realities of her situation. A passport is obtained and she does set out for Saint Petersburg. Her desires, repressed by parental indecision, find a satisfying outlet.

It should be noted, and this is definitely applicable to Prascovie, that obsessional character traits are frequently associated with high ethical standards and these, in turn, have practical value in terms of accomplishment and reliability. Such traits approach the pathologic only when overdeveloped. This is not the case with Prascovie, who has sublimated her tendency to become involved in obsessions. She is not a slave to her irrational impulses, exercises rational control, and, even when obsessional in expressing her wishes, makes her demands in a clear, objective fashion. The authoritarian position taken by her father at first is moderated by a loving attitude. At no time does Prascovie feel she must conceal her desire to go to Saint Petersburg, and she persists in her quest until rewarded with success. Prascovie ostensibly has no need of group therapy since her religious views, and those around her who share them, provide a community of support. What might have been a negative impulse, a repressed feeling of frustration about and resentment of paternal inflexibility, is sublimated by a calm, steady insistence that wins the desired consent at last. The result is a state of mental exaltation that furnishes the inner resources essential to a successful undertaking. Without extensive analysis, Xavier has given a character study of a young girl who could easily have succumbed to external forces to become hopelessly psychotic. Instead, she capitalized on the strength of her obsessions to triumph over her environment. High ethical standards faithfully observed were the key to a happy solution to her dilemma.

Thus, even in applying some of the criteria of modern psychiatry, Xavier's heroine does not fare badly. Adhering scrupulously to his notion of an objective treatment, the author presents a character of several dimensions, but still not an overly complicated one. Her actions and motives are colored by her religious beliefs, which, however, do not get out of hand and result in serious mental disturbance and behavioral disorders. Xavier leaves readers with a limited, yet logical, portrait drawn from real life. Whether a reader's interpretation of Prascovie is theological or is based on present-day psychiatry, her conduct and course of action are in the main justifiable and understandable.

CHAPTER 7

Miscellaneous Writings

I Introduction and Background

E UGÈNE Réaume published the *Oeuvres inédites de Xavier de Maistre* in two volumes in 1877 with Alphonse Lemerre in Paris. Besides over one hundred until then unpublished letters, the edition included fragments of unfinished works: *Histoire d'un prisonnier français; Catherine Freminski; Histoire de Madame Prélestinoff; Histoire racontée au Comte Xavier de Maistre; Un Orage; Une Évasion.* Poems by Xavier are included in Réaume's edition and in Berthier's study. Owing to limitations of space, this chapter concentrates on the *Histoire d'un prisonnier francais*, the best organized in structure and style of the prose fragments. Among examples of Xavier's poetry a few of his versions of Krylov's fables are examined.

II Histoire d'un prisonnier français

The *Histoire d'un prisonnier français* has two main divisions: in the first part is the description of Mme Ardenieff, her immediate family and friends, and the serfs she governs; in the second portion of the story, the unnamed French prisoner relates his sufferings prior to capture by peasants under Mme Ardenieff's jurisdiction. The first half of the *Histoire* is noteworthy for the information it provides on Xavier's political philosophy.

Eager to poke fun at partisans of democracy, Xavier asserts that serfs, contrary to popular belief, are not oppressed by a medieval system of peonage, but enjoy an unrecognized degree of liberty: "One sees by this short exposé that a land in the district is a veritable republic of free slaves. These two words, that perhaps have never been joined together till now, describe rather well, nevertheless, the existence of Russian peasants in the district."[1]

Xavier nonchalantly makes out the institution of serfdom to be no more burdensome than the constitutional monarchy of England. To Xavier there is clearly no basic difference:

. . . Their slavery consists only in not being able to change masters, whom most of them do not know, and not being able to abandon their country; in this way they differ from the English whose liberty consists mainly in being able to leave England, a privilege they use extensively. The serfs can leave their villages anyway and scatter themselves in all the cities of Russia, where they hope to find some advantage, provided that they pay their quota of taxes. . . .[2]

Xavier, fed up with the French Revolution, which he felt spawned Bonaparte, endeavors almost maliciously to demonstrate that a smoothly functioning monarchy has all the advantages of a republic with none of its drawbacks. His defense of an absolute regime could easily be interpreted as sarcasm were it not for solid documentation in his correspondence that he spoke in all seriousness.

There may be some truth in Xavier's insistence that the serfs' lot in Russia was far better than what peasants endured in medieval times or in ancient Greece. In defending his thesis on the leniency of the Russian system, he is most effective when citing the example of Mme Ardenieff, a benevolent governor of the type of district he describes. The charitable attitude of Mme Ardenieff toward all men is revealed in her command to the peasants to spare the hapless French soldier who has fallen into their hands: " 'My children,' she said to the crowd that surrounded him, 'I beseech you, do not commit an evil act by killing an unarmed man; our brave soldiers who took him prisoner could have killed him legally; they did not do so, and now you want to take the life of a poor Christian, who can no longer harm you!' "[3]

Compassion combined with strict justice when necessary is the key to Mme Ardenieff's success as a ruler and to the love and respect she inspires in her people. Indifference on the serfs' part to paying just taxes moves her to take severe measures to insure payment. Mme Ardenieff reaches this decision, Xavier hastens to explain, after due deliberation. The peasants' abuse of her good offices has been a longstanding blot on the relationship between them:

For some years, my children, I have been very unhappy with you. I hear only complaints and murmurs, and I myself have to complain with justice of your inaccuracy; all your payments are delayed, and I am still waiting for last year's deficit that you had promised to pay at the last harvest. Now, to rid you and me of the embarrassment in which we find ourselves, I have decided to take over the land and to have it run by my intendent. . . .[4]

It does not require too long a period for the peasants to size up the situation and yield. Under the absolutist system enforced in Russia, Mme Ardenieff was acting fairly, even though a bit arbitrarily by democratic standards. From this standpoint Xavier's insistence on the benefits of serfdom appears none too convincing. Still, Mme Ardenieff was probably, for the times at least, a paragon of equity. Her ability to commiserate with suffering humanity overshadows any autocratic aspects of her character and, in a measure, substantiates that portion of Xavier's political thesis pertaining to the innate fairness of Russian aristocrats in a position of authority. The good lady's charity, which extends even to the enemies of her country furnishes irrefutable proof of her extraordinary virtue and magnanimity. Xavier lends his characters credibility by a clever use of understatement, thus allowing readers to draw their own conclusions. Mme Ardenieff attains reality in the readers' eyes through what she herself does and says.

The characterization of the nameless French soldier succeeds for much the same reasons. His instinctive reticence and modesty are evinced when he is asked about the circumstances under which he learned to speak Russian. A period of his life, which possibly might have been elucidated if the *Histoire d'un prisonnier français* had been completed, is quickly passed over, leaving the matter to the individual reader's speculation. He hints at an episode that may have involved a broken love affair or political intrigue: " 'I lived,' he said after a moment of silence and indecision, 'two years in the interior of Russia and in Moscow; do not be surprised if your request seemed to trouble me; it recalled to me sad memories and events that I would like to keep to myself and whose story will never come from my lips.' "[5]

The generosity of many Russians toward French soldiers captured in the fighting forms one of the main themes in the story. Like many other emotions experienced in combat by the average foot soldier it is not forgotten, anymore than is the effect that battle fatigue has upon an individual's religious convictions and commitments. In an especially moving passage the prisoner describes his own unforgettable reactions to the prospect of impending death:

> . . . I experienced a feeling of pity for myself which was not without charm; a kind of dream, a mild delirium brought back to me the laughing countryside of my homeland, and focused my thoughts on a thousand disparate objects. I had neither fear of death nor regret of life; I thought untroubled about the eternity that was going to begin for me; religious feelings that have never left me also came to my aid. I did not pray, for I had neither the desire nor the will; the idea of appearing before God, this idea, that in the state of health often made me reflect on my conduct, produced in my heart a movement of confidence and hope whose memory will never leave me.[6]

The intensely warm and vital insights Xavier provides into the mind of a weary soldier resigned to death is a milestone, in its way, in the evolution of literary treatment of the psychology of human beings exposed to the horrors of war. Stendhal, in the *Chartreuse de Parme*, developed this theme in greater detail. In the *Histoire d'un prisonner français*, the title character is the spokesman of Xavier's views on Napoleon's invasion of Russia, with its concomitant suffering and tragedy. Just as Mme Ardenieff embodies the best traditions of Russian aristocracy, so does the prisoner frequently voice Xavier's concern for peace. In the agonizing trek through the snow, captor and captive undergo the same hardships. Finally circumstances oblige the Russians to abandon the French to their fate. Left to shift for themselves, the hapless stragglers come upon an eerie harbinger of imminent doom: " . . . We could then see what threatened us. We were emaciated from starvation; we saw in the distance something black on the snow, but it was a horse dead and already decayed; drawing closer, a cloud of ravens abandoned it and flew in a circle over our heads in order to fight with us for this horrible prey."[7]

A painter's eye is required to seize the visually terrifying features of this shocking scene. The haunting symbolism of the dark cloud of ravens brings to mind Joseph de Maistre's preoccupation with the *bourreau*, the executioner in the *Soirées de Saint-Pétersbourg*. Unquestionably Xavier's contact with Joseph affected his views on war in general as an instrument used by God in requiring atonement for the sins of humanity.

Probing further into the mentality of the soldier in a defeated army, Xavier examines another familiar and painful experience, the death of a comrade-in-arms, when the prisoner recalls the horrifying discovery of the body of a friend:

. . . I noticed then that my comrade Miron was no longer with us. I looked for him in the section of the deserted village where I had seen him walking and I did not delay in finding him. The poor fellow had fallen over some beams and debris which were still burning, his clothes were half consumed; he was dead; I had difficulty recognizing him. He was the only man of our troop in whom I had any interest.[8]

Reduced to the last extremity, the French prisoner is rescued by Mme Ardenieff. Xavier's graphic account of one soldier's experiences, caught in a vise, as it were, between hostile troops and a forbidding climate, is sufficient for a gripping short story. By adding Mme Ardenieff's relations with her peasants, the narrative is expanded in scope and approaches the dimensions of a novelette. A limited amount of local color is inserted by Xavier to convey an adequate impression of what life was like on Mme Ardenieff's estate. The serfs, reluctant to pay any more than necessary to Mme Ardenieff, pursue a tight-fisted policy in dealing with her. A fairly just arrangement to rebuild houses in the village that had been destroyed by a recent fire is greeted with resentment. To the wily farmers, the whole world is a bargaining counter. Unluckily for them, Mme Ardenieff is also an old hand at the game:

This reasonable proposition was received with all the signs of despair, and as an impossible measure to carry out; the moaning and the complaints renewed; the peasants, gathered in different groups, surrounded for the whole day the house where their mistress was, who refused until the eve of her departure to hear them. In spite of their dissatisfaction, they did not fail to bring to Mme Ardenieff poultry, young pigs, eggs, and other foodstuffs.[9]

The foregoing detail is the type Mérimée would be eager to supply since it served what he considered the proper function of local color. As stated previously Xavier foresaw the value of techniques later employed effectively by Mérimée. A case in point and one applicable to the *Histoire d'un prisonnier français* is the use of a physical object that plays an important role in the development of the plot. The two calling cards belonging to Mme Ardenieff and found in the French soldier's possession are a source of suspense and amusement. The kindly aristocrat herself is amazed and intrigued and an atmosphere of speculation and expectation is

created: ". . . Her astonishment was greater still when the woman
handed over to her the military service booklet found on the
prisoner, in which when paging through it she saw two calling cards
with her own name, Madame Ardenieff, in bold letters. . . ."[10]

At last the mystery is solved at the close of the prisoner's tale of
his adventures. The French soldier relates how he discovered a
carriage loaded with plunder from Moscow; it had been abandoned
by some of Napoleon's troops on the approach of the Russians:
"Searching the pockets of the carriage I found the calling cards that
caused you surprise and I put them in my service booklet," he explains. To which Mme Ardenieff, her fears now allayed, replies
philosophically: "We will have many other setbacks when we return
to Moscow."[11]

Sympathetic minor characters are easily recognizable for what
they are. The brave Orthodox priest risks injury by striving to
protect the French soldier and the mayor is appropriately obse-
quious and officious. A significant supporting role is played by
Olga, Mme Ardenieff's daughter. Pretty and impulsive, she is attracted to the Frenchman early in the story. A typical adolescent,
she is enthused about the prospect of a visit to Saint Petersburg
promised by her mother after the cessation of hostilities:

> This hope made her daughter feel a tingling of pleasure; she wrapped
> herself in her fur; she had the impression the fur was lighter and that the
> pace of the sleigh had become faster. But her imagination and her heart
> went more swiftly than the horses; an ardent desire, although still without
> purpose, the confused dream of a happiness to come, one of these bright
> dreams one only has at sixteen, that last for so short a time and are never
> realized, occupied all her thoughts.[12]

Repeatedly assuming the role of literary trailblazer, Xavier
demonstrates his uncanny ability to ferret out subject matter as yet
not fully exploited by writers. In this instance he hits upon the psychology of the adolescent. Later on in the nineteenth century
George Sand was to complain about the lack of attention paid to
teenagers. Olga's reactions are studied and, in passing, Xavier notes
certain adolescent traits and faithfully records them. The dream
world of the sixteen year old in all its unaffected and wide-eyed
wonderment is presented with sensitivity.

The portrayal of Olga as an adolescent type is only one
facet of Xavier's technique in the *Historie d' un prisonnier français*
that casts him in the role of precursor. Together with *La*

Jeune Sibérienne and the *Prisonniers du Caucase*, the *Histoire* rounds out his perception of Russian life, people, and customs. This fact alone, especially in view of the quality of his writing, singles Xavier out as a unique contributor to Franco-Russian literary relations in advancing the importance of Russia in European literature. Whatever he treats is done efficiently and with authenticity. A brief sketch of the system of serfdom and its effect on masters and subjects is meaningful and informative. Intimate glimpses are afforded of everyday life in Russia. Human nature is depicted with thoughtful objectivity, both good and bad points being presented in proper perspective. Above all, Xavier explores knowingly and with great feeling the reactions of soldiers under stress in combat, a foretoken of Stendhal's penetrating analysis in *La Chartreuse de Parme.* Touching as he does on Bonaparte's retreat from Moscow, Xavier prefigures as well the insights of Tolstoi in *War and Peace.* What the finished product might have been if Xavier had completed the *Histoire d'un prisonnier français* is a stimulating subject for speculation.

III   *Xavier's Poetry*

What is in all probability the best lyric poem to be composed by Maistre has a definite connection with Lamartine. Berthier quotes in its entirety a poem ostensibly written in Switzerland by Lamartine in the general period of 1814 when he fled there to escape service in Napoleon's army. The poem in question, "L'Hirondelle," published much later in the *Confidences*, was originally dedicated to a Mlle de Vincy. Of particular interest to Berthier are the first three stanzas of "L'Hirondelle":

Why do you flee me, transient swallow? Come rest your wings next to me. Why flee me? A heart is calling to you. Am I not a wanderer like you?
Fate brings us together in this wilderness. Go, do not be afraid to nestle next to me. If you wail, we shall wail together. Am I not isolated like you?
Perhaps, alas, from the roof that saw you born a cruel fate chases you as it does me. Come take shelter in the wall of my window. Am I not exiled like you?[13]

Xavier's poem, "L'Exilé et l'Hirondelle," has, according to Berthier, a similar theme of exile and concerns the author's stay in Russia, far removed from Sardinia. At one point, Berthier calculates, the two poets may hve compared notes, probably when Lamartine visited Xavier at Bissy. The exchange of ideas for a poem might have taken place in one of two ways. Either Lamartine or Xavier wrote a poem first. Hence one inspired the other, Lamartine exercising an influence on Xavier or vice versa. Another possibility advanced by Berthier is that Xavier wrote his version after having read Lamartine's in the *Confidences*. Be that as it may, the similarity in theme and style is obvious, as a comparison of the first three stanzas of "L'Exilé et l'Hirondelle" with those of "L'Hirondelle" discloses:

Why flee me, transient swallow? Come rest your wing near me. Why flee me when your friend calls you? Am I not a wanderer like you?

Without doubt, far from the shores that saw you born, a cruel fate chases you as it does me. Come put your nest under my window. Am I not exiled like you?

In this wilderness destiny brings us together. Go, do not fear remaining here with me. If you wail, we will wail together. Am I not unhappy like you?[14]

There is no question that Xavier took definite liberties with Lamartine's poem. In fact, he stopped short of being an outright copycat. Plagiarism, however, would be too harsh a charge since Xavier evidently had no intention of publishing his poem. Instead of plagiarism, his version represents an unconscious tribute to Lamartine. To Xavier's credit, the last two stanzas of "L'Exilé et l'Hirondelle" show more originality:

When spring returns to smile on us, you will leave both your refuge and me. You will fly to the country of the zephyr. Alas! Can I not fly there with you!

You will see your first country again, the first nest of your loves, and I—A jealous fate enchains my life here. Am I not to be pitied more than you?[15]

IV   *Versions of Krylov's Fables*

In his versions of Krylov's fables, Xavier faithfully preserved the incisiveness of the verbal barbs originally directed by Krylov against the czarist regime as well as at the everyday shortcomings of fellow Russians. Krylov himself had translated some of La Fontaine's fables. For this reason Xavier would feel at home in finding an appropriate equivalent in French for both the language and spirit of the Russian fabulist. Krylov also had another trait in common with French Classicism; he did not indulge in overproduction, but limited his output to eight or nine fables a year. This schedule allowed ample time for careful reworking and furbishing of lines. A few examples of Xavier's fables adapted from Krylov suffice to show the success of the former's efforts.

"L'Habit de Janot" is an obvious commentary on the mismanagement of an individual's affairs, which are compared to a suit of clothes. Janot, the ne'er-do-well, is a witty fellow dressed in rags with his elbows coming out at the sleeves. To fix his sleeves, Janot cuts the bottom part from his coat to use as patching material. The results are ludicrous, for now the coat is too short for the rest of his garments. Undismayed, Janot enunciates a carefree philosphy: "Oh, well! In my mind I have more than one resource. I am going to repair it all without unfastening my pursestrings!"[16]

"Les Paysans et le fleuve" relates an incident that might well refer either to the plight of peasants under the Bourbons or the serfs under the czars. In this case the protagonist is a river, not a lion or a wolf, that is the bane of the distraught farmers. Flooded fields and damaged property oblige them to hold a meeting to solve their dilemma. Since the monarch was an unlikely source of help only one alternative remained: "Obtaining help was always difficult and the poor injured person did not approach the palace of his kings without fear. Let us address our grievance to the River into whom our floods have returned! He reigns as sovereign over the turbulent water. . . ."[17] The peasants to their consternation behold the River silently and ruthlessly sweeping still further over their lands. Crushed by the relentless forces of nature, they sadly realize the utter hopelessness of their situation. All stronger powers work in collusion against them.

Humans like to think they can dominate animals, but in "Le Chevalier errant et son cheval" the tables are turned. Confident of cajoling his faithful steed into yet another perilous mission fraught with hardships, the knight with incredible unction holds out promises of rewards in which the noble horse will share: "When through your help and great prowess helping everywhere the widow and orphan, I have conquered more than one kingdom, you will no longer graze, as you do now, on the thatch which serves as a roof to the house."[18] The horse has heard this speech once too often and his dignified silence is unanswerable.

Another lesson is taught in "Le Berger et le moucheron." A shepherd sleeps peacefully, unaware that a poisonous snake is about to strike. Fortunately, a friendly gnat sees the danger and takes steps to warn the shepherd: "But, happily, a cousin perceives the peril of the herdsman without defense, and, seized with pity, darts rapidly right into the sleeper's ear. Singing, buzzing there, he makes a big noise to arouse the imprudent man from his peaceful sleep."[19] Abruptly awakened, the shepherd kills the snake but also squashes the friendly gnat buzzing in his ear. Unsolicited warnings frequently provoke a violent reaction.

The fickleness that underlies alleged friendships is the theme of "L'Amitié des chiens." Two dogs vow eternal comradeship to one another. They have so much in common there is little reason to suspect any disagreement, not to mention the chance of bitter rivalry. Each strives to outdo the other in a cloying expression of mutual esteem: "If, for example, we live here in this way, both destined to guard the same door, affable to one another, cordial, generous, could we not spend happy days in peace? When people love each other they are all that way!"[20] Saccharine outpourings of trust and admiration abruptly cease when a bone is tossed to the dogs. Hunger overrides their lofty sentiments and they go at each other's throats in a vicious fight over food, a basic everyday necessity more important to them now than a lasting friendship. What can be said of dogs applies quite aptly to human society.

Krylov, who set rigorous standards for his profession, would have been satisfied with Xavier's interpretation of his poems. The Sardinian did not stoop to servile imitation, but endeavored, in a clear and rhythmical style in French, to preserve the spirit of Krylov. In any assessment of Xavier's adaptations of Krylov it is useful to compare his work with a two volume study, *Fables Russes de M. Kriloff*, published in Paris in 1825 by Count Orloff. Xavier is not mentioned, although several names popular in the heyday of French Romanticism but long since forgotten are listed along with their translations of some of Krylov's fables. Secondary writers like Casimir Delavigne, Viennet, Soumet, and Sophie and Delphine Gay present their efforts, which pale by comparison to Xavier's sprightly lines. Only in 1860 did Alfred Bougeault, in *Kryloff, sa vie et ses fables*, give a long overdue, albiet brief, recognition, to Xavier's interpretation of the Russian fabulist.[21]

CHAPTER 8

Xavier's Literary Reputation

I Xavier Viewed by Other Writers

AMONG contemporaries of Xavier no one made more unusual comments than Stendhal who concluded that the "likeable author of the *Voyage*" scarcely resembled Joseph, noted for his "tender friendship with the executioner." Branding the elder Maistre a Jesuitical reactionary, Stendhal blamed Joseph for the restoration of a vindictive autocracy in France. All the two brothers had in common was "a good deal of wit." There the similarity ended.[1]

Stendhal's Anglophile bias is very much in evidence when comparing Xavier to Sterne. The *Voyage* was a mediocre work "an imitation of Sterne, but an imitation without depth and without genius." Stendhal must have read the *Voyage* hurriedly; the remark that Xavier "imitates Sterne constantly and never talks about him" suggests a rapid scanning of a few pages chosen at random. Totally oblivious to the innovative aspects of the *Voyage*, Stendhal dismisses the work contemptuously as an example of "the little literature" of the period just before the Revolution. It is amazing, therefore, to find Stendhal doing a *volte-face* to praise the *Expédition*, "very superior to the first part, a very rare accident in literature."[2] The only sections of the *Voyage* of any merit consisted of occasional passages on the fair sex, a patent borrowing from Sterne in Stendhal's opinion. The exquisite world of fantasy and the pursuit of the feminine ideal were ostensibly beyond the sharp-tongued critic's comprehension.

Le Lépreux was only noted in passing, but Stendhal has favorable things to say about the *Prisonniers* and *La Jeune Sibérienne*. The tale concerning the Caucasus and the Chechens is admired for its picturesque details, although there is no analysis whatsoever of Xavier's startling characterization of Ivan. The comment, "It is

131

Walter Scott arranged for the tastes of an amiable court,"[3] is hardly perceptive, as Stendhal betrays too hasty a perusal of another of Xavier's works.

La Jeune Sibérienne is the one tale that Stendhal took the time to digest. "The philosopher who derives pleasure from divining the hidden forces of men's actions" as well as the casual reader satisfied by "two hours of sweet emotion in a little book" would both heartily applaud Xavier's efforts. It is surprising in the first place that Stendhal found anything at all to praise in a tale with decided religious overtones. Even more unexpected is his appraisal of Prascovie; he was exuberant about her courage in boldly demanding permission from her father to leave Siberia and visit the czar. "She demonstrates energetically . . . the greatest obstacles encountered by extraordinary projects." Stendhal always had respect for forceful women and undeniably this is his estimate of Prascovie. The conclusion of the brief analysis of Prascovie does not conform to the usual Stendhalean norms; the heroine of *La Jeune Sibérienne* proves that, motivated by "*Love of God* . . . man's strength can be increased a hundredfold."[4] No mention is made of her subsequent decision to enter the convent and undoubtedly Stendhal would have preferred to end the tale with Prascovie's success at the Russian court; some of his most vigorous feminine types evolved from a convent background into bold and uninhibited *beylistes*.

Stendhal's own preconceptions affected his assessment of Xavier. A "nuance of Italian taste" and "Italian finesse"[5] were noted in Xavier by Stendhal, himself fond of Italy and its culture. In the political aspects of the *Prisonniers* and *La Jeune Sibérienne* Stendhal treats Xavier's acceptance of czarist depotism with considerable understanding and recognizes the author's difficult position as an aristocrat fearful of harshly criticizing his adopted country. A second version of *La Jeune Sibérienne*, to be published posthumously, would have been, Stendhal suggests, a brave and necessary gesture on Xavier's part with a vivid revelation of all the cruelty of exile in Siberia.

Much as Stendhal dislikes provincialism in any form, he surmises that a prolonged residence in Paris would have robbed Xavier's writings of their wit and originality, a notion he may well have expressed to Mérimée, whose own narrative technique and structure parallel those of Xavier. In view of Stendhal's enthusiasm over the *Prisonniers* and *La Jeune Sibérienne*, it is conceivable he would have discussed the merits of Xavier with Mérimée; this would seem the most likely connection between Mérimée and Xavier.

There was never any question about the enthusiasm with which Lamartine greeted the works of Xavier. A close friend of Louis de Vignet, a nephew of Xavier, the poet recalls how they read with other friends the *Lépreux*, "the supreme sorrow of isolation in martyrdom" expressed in a manner worthy of the Bible. "We were acquainted in this genre," Lamartine reminisces in the *Cours familier de littérature*, "only with the lyrical accent of the prophet, of Job and Chateaubriand." The *Night Thoughts* of Young, Goethe's *Werther, Atala,* and *René* could affect the sensibilities of young Romantics of Lamartine's generation but he found something more in *Le Lépreux*, "not just the declamation of the writer, but the very impression of the one who is suffering."[6]

Lamartine also makes passing mention of the *Voyage*, an "enjoyable badinage."[7] The dialogue between the leper and Xavier, however, absorbed most of Lamartine's attention and left its mark on the narrative poem, *Jocelyn*. The leper serves as a model for Jocelyn, who also suffers the pangs of isolation, as a priest separated from a sweetheart by the vow of celibacy. Needless to say, Jocelyn does not represent the solidly Christian resignation of the leper, but the priest's grief and sorrow do ring out in tones often resembling the lamentations of Xavier's character. Jocelyn's attachment to a pet dog and his outlook on nature as an animated entity also bring to mind similar passages in *Le Lépreux*. Other works by Lamartine, particularly *Le Tailleur de pierres de Saint-Point*, have frequent echoes of the leper's religious philosophy and sense of alienation.

Sainte-Beuve, while he infuriated Xavier by erroneous references to the latter's supposed trysts with a lover in the vicinity of the leper's tower, did write a generally thoughtful criticism of him in the *Revue des deux mondes* of 1839. Although Sainte-Beuve recognizes the differences in temperament of the two brothers, he overemphasizes the extent of Joseph's influence on Xavier when the bases for differentiating them should have been clear.

Among the most perceptive comments of Sainte-Beuve, one concerning the *Voyage* is quite provocative inasmuch as the critic finds Xavier's work closer in spirit to Charles Lamb than to Laurence Sterne. (Sainte-Beuve still finds echoes of Sterne in the *Voyage*.) Another aspect of the *Voyage* that catches Sainte-Beuve's attention is the visual quality of the descriptions, traceable to Xavier's background as a painter. The soul-beast relationship is characterized as "sweet malice." In Xavier's reaction to nature Sainte-Beuve senses a Lamartinean melancholy.

The distinguished critic is aware of Xavier's many-sided career in military service, his relations with the Swiss author Töpffer, his fairly successful attempts at poetry, and his versions of Krylov. Most of all Sainte-Beuve admires the *Prisonniers* and *La Jeune Sibérienne* and seems to recognize Xavier's originality in treating Russian subjects. As he so often does, Sainte-Beuve falls back on the theory of the *famille des esprits*, writers of kindred tendencies, to observe keenly, "People scarcely expect me to compare M. Xavier de Maistre to M. Mérimée: they are the two most perfect we have, the two most skillful, the former in copying the true, the latter in representing it." Sainte-Beuve proceeds to assure readers he acknowledges Mérimée's superiority in depth and insight but, nevertheless, credits Xavier with an indefinable quality of humanity and a lack of affectation. "M. Mérimée," Sainte-Beuve wagers, "might envy this characterization of Ivan, of this brave servant of the major, at once so faithful and so ferocious."

Le Lépreux and *La Jeune Sibérienne* are also commended by Sainte-Beuve for their directness and unpretentiousness in dealing with actual persons and events. Prascovie's criticism of painting that does not depict truthfully things as they really exist sums up precisely, to Sainte-Beuve's satisfaction, the essence of Xavier's art.

Throughout much of the nineteenth century Xavier's reputation was obscured by Joseph's stature. Occasional references with brief but due recognition of his contributions can be found in standard histories of French literature. Louis Veuillot, a rabid Catholic critic, alluded to Joseph often in his correspondence but did not mention Xavier. In the twentieth century a few works have been written on Xavier and some writers have acknowledged his importance in French letters. Anatole France judged him "a little too innocent" to be a close facsimile of Sterne. "The tone of the *Voyage autour de ma chambre* passes from a moderate sprightliness to a restrained melancholy without ever going to extremes";[9] this is a fitting resumé of France's amiable appriasal of Xavier.

Henry Bordeaux in 1930 discovered much to appreciate in *Le Lépreux*. His comments provide an appropriate summary of Xavier's present status in French literature: " . . . The art of Xavier is delicate and subtle although it seems a little passé. It resembles those withered flowers that retain a surprising fragrance. They are believed to be dead, and their fragrant little spirit persists in living. . . . However, from these unpretentious little writings a very sharp expression of reality and truth stands out. . . ."[10]

II *Some Disciples and Imitators of Xavier*

Almost totally neglected in the overview of Xavier's impact on the writers of his generation is the effect of the *Voyage* and *Expédition* on a widely read work in America in the 1850s, *Reveries of a Bachelor*. Today the name of Donald Grant Mitchell, who wrote under the pen name of "Ik Marvel," has little meaning to students of American letters, with the exception of specialists. Yet at one time the *Reveries* was a popular book that went into any number of editions. Authors of the caliber of Emily Dickinson read Mitchell with enthusiasm. Of significance to comparatists are the numerous references to French *litterateurs* in the *Reveries*, an insertion that was not the unpredictable whim of a rambunctious author. No stranger to French belles-lettres, Mitchell had lived and studied in France, and was, moreover, quite familiar with the tastes and interests of the informed reading public most likely to purchase his book. French was then the second language of the educated, and translations of the latest works from France were selling like hotcakes. The novels of George Sand and the prose works of Lamartine were on the shelves of many private and public libraries.[11]

Mitchell was not an isolated francophile, for he found plenty of company in New York's most prestigious and intellectually invigorating salon. The hostess was Anne Lynch Botta, who had an international reputation as one of the moving forces in the New York literati and was a leader of the francophiles there. Poe and Emerson were frequent guests at her home and almost every celebrity passing through the city was lionized in a reception in her drawing rooms. At Mrs. Botta's Mitchell would naturally be encouraged to include frequent mention of France and its literature in the *Reveries*.

Mitchell had little need of acquainting readers with the author of the *Voyage* and *Expédition*. Translations of his works had appeared much earlier in America and without question many readers of the *Reveries* had already studied Xavier in class, for French was a standard subject in the curriculum of seminaries and universities. A reference, then, to Xavier in the *Reveries* came as no surprise. Difficulty in lighting a fire causes Mitchell to think of his French colleague in similar circumstances during the course of a room journey. The *Reveries* were essentially a series of armchair reminiscences and imaginary travels in the Maistrean manner, so mention of Xavier was in order: "It does not burn freely, so I put on the blower. Quaint and good-natured Xavier de Maistre would have made, I dare say, a pretty epilogue about a sheet-iron blower but I cannot."[12]

Adhering to the general outlines of the *Voyage* and *Expédition*, Mitchell in the preface strikes a Maistrean note when announcing to readers that the *Reveries* are "whimseys and reflections, as a great many brother bachelors are apt to indulge in, but which they are too cautious, or too prudent, to lay before the world."[13] Parallels between the *Reveries* and Xavier's works may be seen in the American author's reflections on life around him. An urban flat provides a locale far removed from rural solitude. Confronted with a large city, Mitchell's observations approximate those of Xavier in the *Expédition*, isolated in an attic on a side street in Turin: "But I am in a garret of the city. From my window I look over a mass of crowded house-tops—moralizing often upon the scene, but in a strain too long and sombre to be set down here. In place of the wide country chimney, with its iron fire-dogs, is a snug grate, where the maid makes me a fire in the morning and rekindles it in the afternoon."[14]

"Ik Marvel" also implied that the crowded circumstances of metropolitan living could easily arouse him to dash off a series of sober and critical reflections on mass society. Both Mitchell and Xavier viewed the social scene with the air of the country gentleman. The American was somewhat more democratic by comparison but not excessively republican, a term tantamount to communist in those days in the United States. Mitchell, as a news reporter in Paris, witnessed the turmoil in 1848 during Lamartine's ill-fated regime and had no stomach for uncontrolled popular rule. His reactions to revolutions in France would by and large agree with Xavier's views.

Mitchell did not brood for long on gloomy topics and shared Xavier's interest in womanly pulchritude, an exhilarating object of contemplation for the American author whether outdoors or indoors. Before the fireplace with the flickering flames enabling him to lapse peacefully into a reverie, he dreams about a former sweetheart with the commonplace name of Nelly. She lacks the imperiousness of Mme de Hautcastel but otherwise has the prettiness Xavier expected in his girl friends: " . . . Her charms steal over you gently, and almost imperceptibly. . . . And you keep studying what on earth it can be that makes you so earnest to be near her, or to listen to her voice. . . . Upon a sudden, some fine day, when the air is balmy still, you wonder if you are in love. . . ."[15]

Nelly is converted into a general symbol of the feminine ideal, the object of Mitchell's meditations interspersed through the *Reveries*. This aspect of Mitchell's work resembles Xavier's technique more closely than other motifs in the *Reveries*, although the American writer is not prepared to probe into all the psychological ramifications of his dreams about fair ladies; his connection with Xavier provides a fascinating episode in Franco-American literary relations.

In Switzerland the *Voyage* and *Expédition* influenced the writing of an engaging author, Rudolph Töpffer, who carried on a lively correspondence with Xavier. In one of Töpffer's tales, *Le Grand Saint-Bernard*, there is a direct reference to *Le Lépreux*. The collection of Töpffer's stories and essays, *Nouvelles Genevoises*, possesses a nonchalance and ease that recall the best moments of the *Expédition* and the *Voyage*.[16] *La Bibliothèque de mon oncle*, in particular, parallels these two works of Xavier in theme and style. The tale concerns Jules, a young lad who has no family except a kindly and eccentric uncle with a library from which the neighbors all borrow books. Jules grows up to be a painter with Xavier's penchant for daydreaming. Although Jules does not engage in room travel, he focuses his mind on thoughts and fancies similar to those entertained by the Sardinian writer: great authors of the past, fair ladies, his immediate surroundings, the persons about him. Jules creates a dreamlike atmosphere interwoven throughout the fabric of *La Bibliothèque de mon oncle* and in Maistrean fashion invites the reader to participate vicariously in the action.

Longing to be a poet, Jules has as well the eye of a painter, and the gorgeous view from his room moves him, as a similar panorama did Xavier, in the *Expédition*, to describe the beauties of nature. The reaction of Jules, as often witnessed in Xavier, is one of melancholy, for the scene evokes sad feelings and emotions characteristic of a Romantic poet with the visual acuteness of a painter. Peering out his window one day Jules espies a fetching miss on her way to borrow a book from his uncle. She remains in the background in much the same manner as Xavier's bewitching neighbor in the *Expédition*. While Töpffer touches on the subject of beautiful ladies that occupy Jules' thoughts, there is no recurrent theme of the ideal lady haunting Jules' dreams and persistently present in the subconscious. Unlike Xavier, Jules finally meets at the end of the narrative Henriette, the girl he is to marry. She remains very much a reality and does not become a fleeting vision.

A contemporary of Xavier, although much younger by several decades, wrote a work along the general lines of the *Voyage autour de ma chambre*. Alphonse Karr's *Voyage autour de mon jardin* (1845)[17] imitates not only the title of Xavier's book but is an effort to create a similar blithe air of fantasy and to indulge in discursive reflections on plants, insects, life, love, and what not. The references to flora and fauna soon become tedious and only a few pages capture for a brief moment some of the spontaneity of Xavier's *Voyage*. Karr was known as a French writer in the tradition of Laurence Sterne, but the *Voyage autour de mon jardin* did little to justify that distinction. A monthly publication, the *Guêpes*, notorious for its satirical barbs, represents probably his best work.

III   *Sterne and Xavier*

There is some similarity between Sterne and Xavier in family background. Both writers had fathers who enjoyed a patriarchal role. Yet there are points of difference. Xavier was firmly opposed to dueling, a barbaric practice about which Sterne had no strong feelings one way or the other. The same principle obtains in their religious upbringing. Sterne, who was ordained an Anglican priest, was indebted to his uncle, the Canon of York, for a certain status in the Church of England, but piety was of little concern to Sterne. Xavier's religious formation was rigorous by contrast although, even with priests in the immediate family, his adherence to Catholicism increased in fervor only in later life. As for love affairs, Sterne's amorous conquests are a matter of open record. While there is reason to suspect that the references to Mme de Hautcastel in the *Voyage* are the façade for a not entirely Platonic association, Xavier's discretion contrasts markedly with Sterne's flippancy on sexual matters.

The French writer was a young soldier at the time of the composition of the *Voyage* whereas Sterne was more mature, experienced, and past fifty when he wrote *Sentimental Journey*. If Xavier had authored the *Voyage* later in life, the contrast between the two writers would have been striking indeed for Maistre grew more reactionary and conservative with the passing of the years.

In more than one instance there are points in Sterne's *Sentimental Journey* and *Tristram Shandy* that bear some similarity to episodes in Xavier's *Voyage* and *Expédition*. Maistre's remonstrance with Joannetti for helping a beggar seems inspired to some extent by Yorick's rebuke of the monk and subsequent remorse for this uncharitable outburst in the *Sentimental Journey*. La Fleur, Yorick's footman, is more merry and worldlywise than the compliant Joannetti. Not satisfied with performing routine duties, La Fleur, on the road with Yorick, makes friends easily with kitchen workers at the inns where they are lodged and regales them with a fife. The brief encounter of Xavier with a fair neighbor recapitulates Yorick's meeting with the comely wife of a Parisian shopkeeper in the course of which the husband catches Yorick in the compromising act of holding the lady's wrist.

The roguish licentiousness and amorality in *Sentimental Journey* contrasts sharply with the more polished and courtly air of the *Voyage* and *Expédition*. Xavier goes to great lengths to approach pretty damsels with all due propriety, whereas Yorick proceeds from a casual encounter to a boudoir rendezvous without batting an eye. Mme de Hautcastel is addressed by Xavier in the politest of terms even when in disagreement. Madame de Rambouliet, a French lady of Yorick's acquaintance, is scarcely the delicate type. She decorously requests Yorick to stop the coach in which they are riding, and informs him in gutter language she has to relieve herself. Xavier is not above playing the sly rascal now and then, but Yorick's total lack of inhibitions in calling a spade a spade is foreign to the Sardinian writer's nature.

Sterne alludes blandly from time to time to the ground covered in his travels (which are not fanciful room journeys) with a leisurely and sprightly air not at all conducive to grim reflections. While Xavier may borrow a few ideas and episodes from Sterne, he definitely alters the tone of the *Voyage* and *Expédition* to suit his own temperament. One point, however, raised by Sterne in *Tristram Shandy* may have shaped Xavier's thinking along certain lines. In order to demonstrate the nonsense involved in unduly complicated explanations of the obvious, Tristram distinguishes between two faculties, common in man, and uses two knobs on the back of a chair to illustrate his point: "You see, they are the highest and most ornamental parts of its *frame*,—as wit and judgment are of *ours*,—and like them too, indubitably both made and fitted to go together, in order as we say in all such cases of duplicated embellishments— to answer one another."[18]

Did Xavier hit upon Sterne's distinction in down-to-earth terms between wit and judgment and expand it to a provocative theme for the *Voyage?* Possibly Tristram's humorous remarks inspired in some way the evolution of Xavier's soul-beast relationship. If so, he profited by Sterne's pseudoacademic exposition to develop one of the central motifs of the *Voyage*.

In using Sterne as a model, Xavier was quite successful and compensated in grace and circumspection for what he lacked in Sterne's depth, expansiveness of vision, and understanding of human nature. One point in Xavier's favor and an improvement on Sterne's technique is the probing into dreams and the subconscious coupled with the poetic pursuit of the oneiric vision of the ideal woman.

Sterne and Xavier, like many European authors, borrowed from Ariosto and Cervantes. *Orlando Furioso* supplied motifs in the area of fantasy, beautiful ladies, and magic steeds, but these devices, while they would have some effect on Sterne and an even greater one on Xavier, remained largely conventional and stereotyped. Sterne and Xavier had to develop their respective techniques on their own, the former his free-swinging and far-reaching narrative style, and the latter his more limited yet simultaneously deeper insights into relatively unexplored facets of the psyche.

Ariosto would get the two writers started on the right track, but Cervantes had even more to offer them. In *Don Quixote* a new world was opened to future authors with the imaginative handling of the motif of the feminine ideal pursued in a dreamlike realm. There is a noteworthy difference between Quixote and Xavier; the lovable knight errant begins with a dream and forces it, to his own satisfaction at least, to materialize in reality. Xavier does just the opposite; his reality is transformed into a dream.

Other similarities between Xavier and Quixote give rise to interesting comparisons. The Sardinian in the *Expédition* is perched on a window sill that has become an imaginary steed, recalling Clavileño, the wooden horse on which Quixote takes fanciful trips. Throughout the *Quixote* there is a vigorous defense of the imagination, echoed by Xavier in less declamatory tones; a serious discussion of Platonism in the *Quixote* may have some connection with the soul-beast relationship. Joannetti in a modest way recapitulates, in some disagreements with Xavier, the arguments between the dreamy Don and the pragmatic Sancho Panza; one example involves giving alms to a beggar. It may be said that Quixote almost always breaks the illusion to make it an actuality, whereas Xavier in the *Voyage* seeks to create and maintain it. The Sardinian is indeed quixotic when he reads poetry to an angry neighbor who concludes Xavier has gone mad, a judgment passed continually on Cervantes' hero. Of course the ramifications of Cervantes' profound work ultimately exceed the modest parameters of the *Voyage* and *Expédition*. The fact remains, nonetheless, that *Don Quixote*'s general influence on European literature is not infrequently overlooked.

IV   Xavier and Russia

In Russia under Catherine II there was a growing enthusiasm for French culture. Russian aristocrats and intellectuals discovered in the language and fashions of France a novel and exciting civilization. Upper class children invariably had French tutors and Catherine II's correspondence with the *philosophes* was one of the important developments of the Enlightenment. Diderot was probably the most prestigious visitor from France in the eighteenth century to be received at the court of Catherine II. French culture had a widespread effect on many aspects of Russian life in the eighteenth century in cuisine, clothing, furniture, theater, and manners. More and more French was spoken in the salons and actors from Paris presented the latest plays from the Comédie Française. There was also a strong French influence on Russian education, thanks largely to the efforts of Catherine II.

But if the Russians had been won over to French culture, there was little evidence of a spirit of reciprocity in Paris, where the notion still prevailed that no other civilization could hold a candle to France. Eventually two opposing schools of literature arose in Russia, one decidedly francophile in its orientation and the other concerned with developing a Russian literature based on national themes. With the French Revolution there was at first a wave of admiration in Russia soon followed by bitter disillusionment. Many aristocrats driven from France by the Terror went to Saint Petersburg.

Such was the situation when Joseph and Xavier de Maistre came to Russia. An intermittent state of war between Napoleon and the czar had little effect on Franco-Russian cultural relations. The plays of Racine and Corneille were presented in Saint Petersburg. Vasili Pushkin, uncle of the well-known poet and a writer of some merit, appeared in Molière's comedies, assisted at times by his young nephew, Alexander. The Maistres naturally thrived in such a cultural ambiance and, as French-speaking subjects of an Italian nation allied to the czar, were admirably suited to the sociopolitical climate.

When the fortunes of war turned against Napoleon and led to his defeat by Russia, the czar's troops swarmed into Paris. Unlike the armies of other members of the Coalition, the Russian troops as well as the diplomats proved generous conquerors. Mme de Staël remarked that Russia, of all the European nations, was the only one that did not seem motivated by hatred and a desire for revenge. What the French lost on the battlefield they won back through the impact of French Romanticism on Russian literature. Chateaubriand, Lamartine, and Mme de Staël influenced the rising generation of writers headed by Alexander Pushkin. The latter, although ardently dedicated to the task of producing a native Russian literature, still reflected in his own writings the results of his reading of the French Romantics.

Xavier de Maistre's position as an in-law of Pushkin has received little attention in studies of Franco-Russian literary relations even though both writers composed works on the same general theme—captivity among the wild tribes of the Caucasus. Pushkin's *Prisoner of the Caucasus* appeared in 1822. It is more than a mere coincidence that Xavier's *Prisonniers du Caucase* was published several years before in 1815. Like Xavier, Pushkin had seen service with czarist troops in the Caucasus and left that wild country with visions that somewhere in that free and untamed territory Rousseau's ideal of natural beauty and virtue could be found. His *Prisoner of the Caucasus* is an account of what happens to a disillusioned young intellectual from Saint Petersburg who seeks solitude among the Circassians far removed from the artificiality of urban life. No longer stifled by a conventional existence, the hero, even though taken captive by the Caucasian tribesmen, admires their honesty as opposed to the hypocrisy of presumably civilized society.

Despite the differences in plot, both Xavier and Pushkin furnish an authentic portrait of the picturesque milieu of the Caucasian tribes. In view of their acquaintance with one another and their mutual family ties, what connection is there between the two works other than the similarity in title? While documentary evidence may be lacking, it is not too far-fetched a conjecture to assume that the two writers met at some point and discussed the possibilities of writing a work based on the Caucasian tribes with whom they were both acquainted. Since they may have been writing their respective tales in the same general period, Pushkin, quite possibly, could be indebted to his uncle-in-law for something far more substantive than the title and general subject.

Mention of the *Prisonniers du Caucase* also brings to mind Leo Tolstoi's writings on the Caucasus: *A Raid* (1853), *The Woodfelling* (1855), and *The Cossacks* (1863). Since Xavier wrote his works earlier, might there not be some connection between Xavier's tales on Russian themes and those of Tolstoi? The assumption in view of the circumstances is not highly conjectural.

Some comparisons may also be drawn between Dostoievsky's *House of the Dead* and *La Jeune Sibérienne*. At the time Xavier wrote the story of Prascovie, Russian authors, out of fear of the authorities, refrained from any mention of Siberia. As a foreigner, the Sardinian appears to have escaped rigorous censure. Xavier's descriptions of the prisoners' situation in Siberia were surprisingly accurate. Although Dostoievsky develops this theme in greater depth and detail, Xavier's pioneer role cannot be disregarded.

One fact generally overlooked in studies of Franco-Russian literary relations is the presence of the Maistres in Saint Petersburg, the only French writers of any prominence in the first part of the nineteenth century to take up residence there for an extended period. While Joseph's output was far greater than Xavier's, it was the latter who actually treated Russian themes. From this standpoint Xavier occupies a unique position in the literary history of France and Russia; he was in addition the first French writer of recognized merit and artistry to adapt into French some of the poems of the Russian La Fontaine, Ivan Krylov. [19]

V *Conclusion*

Inevitably Xavier has had to submit time and again to comparison with Joseph, and while the elder Maistre overshadowed his younger brother, the latter did not always fare badly in any close study. Having started a literary career much earlier, Joseph had much to offer Xavier by way of advice. However, it may not be generally known that Joseph gladly accepted suggestions from Xavier in the composition of the *Soirées de Saint-Pétersbourg*, so there was a substantial exchange of counsel and help on both sides. [20] As pointed out in preceding chapters, Xavier eventually adopted Joseph's hard line on Catholicism and monarchy and assimilated a good deal of the apocalyptic spirit of the *Soirées*. Both writers had formidable powers of observation, manifested in their analysis of the world about them. Xavier passed through wider and more varied stages of development than Joseph and, paradoxically, ended by becoming more impersonal in his literary manner. The vigorous individualism in the *Soirées* seems highly subjective when compared with the calm and cool view of reality in the *Prisonniers* and *La Jeune Sibérienne*.

It was this impersonality coupled with the flights of fantasy in his early works that made Xavier such a provocative and far-sighted precursor. Caught up in the first currents of Romanticism, he reacted to the wonders of the physical world with unabashed joy and melancholy. Yet he discovered a deeper phase of the Romantic movement in the exploration of oneiric and subconscious data. *Le Lépreux* represents a midway point between the subjective Romantic and the objective Realist; the leper's situation is, on the one hand, dispassionately analyzed, and, on the other, passionately expressed in an unrestrained outburst of desperation subsequently mitigated by a courageous resignation. Many of these qualities persist throughout the *Prisonniers* and *La Jeune Sibérienne*. In the drama set in the Caucasus the Realism of Xavier is more pungent, with scarcely a trace of the author's personal views or feelings. The elements of personalism and Realism intermingle more freely in the story of Prascovie in which Xavier remains on the whole the disinterested observer.

What might have been the future trends in Xavier's literary evolution are evidenced in the *Histoire d'un prisonnier français* and his poems. He could have become a fair poet and at the very least a promising novelist. In the *Histoire* the psychology of war and its effect on the individual are subjected to keen scrutiny. The treatment of Russian themes and the versions of Krylov's fables add to Xavier's stature as a literary trailblazer. Almost two decades before Mérimée he chanced upon the fresh effects attainable through an impersonal view of reality. In a few tales he demonstrated a surprising ability to treat a variety of themes and character types. One of the most fascinating aspects of Xavier's achievement is the venture into the world of fantasy. In five tales and essays, along with a few miscellaneous writings, Xavier bequeathed quite a heritage to posterity.

Largely forgotten today and remembered on occasion as a sort of literary oddity, Xavier de Maistre stands in need of a wider degree of recognition. It is not rash by any means to conjecture that a reevaluation of his significance in French literature would lead to a renewed study of an additional member of the Maistre family.

Notes and References

Chapter One

1. For further biographical data readers are referred to: Abbé Alfred Berthier, *Xavier de Maistre* (Lyon, 1921); *Oeuvres inédites de Xavier de Maistre*, 2 vols, ed. Eugène Réaume (Paris, 1877); Maurice de la Fuye, *Xavier de Maistre* (Tours, 1934).

2. La Fuye, p. 27. All translations, unless otherwise cited, are my own.

3. *Oeuvres inédites*, II, 103. Hereafter referred to as *O. I.*

4. *Ibid.*, p. 123.

5. Berthier, p. 209. *Bans* was a sobriquet given to Xavier by his family.

6. *Ibid.*, p. 210.

Chapter Two

1. *Oeuvres complètes* de Xavier de Maistre, (Paris, 1862), pp. 43 - 44. Hereafter referred to as *O. C.*

2. *Ibid.*, p. 51.

3. *Ibid.*, p. 80.

4. *Ibid.*, p. 81.

5. *Ibid.*, p. 82.

6. *Ibid.*, p. 83.

7. *Ibid.*, p. 83.

8. *Ibid.*, p. 84.

9. *Ibid.*, pp. 84 - 85.

10. *Ibid.*, p. 46.

11. *Ibid.*, p. 94.

12. *Ibid.*, p. 95.

13. *Ibid.*, p. 20.

14. *Ibid.*, p. 23.

15. *Ibid.*, p. 24.

16. *Ibid.*, p. 35. When wondering about the way Rosine, the affectionate dog, is attracted to him, Xavier speculates: "I would rather believe in Martinism."

17. *Ibid.*, p. 89.

18. *Ibid.*, p. 93.

19. *Ibid.*, p. 108.

20. *Ibid.*, p. 100.

21. *Ibid.*, p. 101.

22. See Pierre-Georges Castex, *Le Conte fantastique en France* (Paris, 1951).

23. *O. C.*, p. 13.

24. *Ibid.*, p. 18.

25. Quoted by Berthier, p. 215.

26. *Ibid.*, pp. 215 - 216.

27. *O. C.*, p. 9.

28. *Ibid.*, p. 15.

29. *Ibid.*, p. 76.

30. *Ibid.*, p. 90.

31. *Ibid.*, p. 70.

32.a *Ibid.*, p. 103.

32.b *Ibid.*, p. 104.

33. *Ibid.*, p. 65.

34. *Ibid.*, p. 67.

35. *Ibid.*, p. 67.

36. *Ibid.*, p. 45.

37. *Ibid.*, p. 45.

38. *Ibid.*, p. 46.

39. *Ibid.*, p. 21.

40. *Ibid.*, p. 57.

41. *Ibid.*, p. 52.

42. *Ibid.*, p. 54.

Chapter Three

1. *O. C.*, p. 114.

2. *Ibid.*, pp. 117 - 18.

3. *Ibid.*, p. 119.

4. *Ibid.*, pp. 122 - 23.

5. *Ibid.*, p. 127.

6. *Ibid.*, p. 129.

7. *Ibid.*, p. 147.

8. *Ibid.*, p. 165.

9. *Ibid.*, p. 151.

10. *Ibid.*, p. 152.

11. *Ibid.*, pp. 134 - 35.

12. *Ibid.*, p. 140.

13. *Ibid.*, p. 141.

14. *Ibid.*, p. 142.

15. *Ibid.*, p. 155.

16. *Ibid.*, pp. 160 - 61.

17. *Ibid.*, p. 116.

18. *Ibid.*, p. 143.

19. *Ibid.*, p. 177.

20. *Ibid.*, p. 184.

21. *Ibid.*, p. 185.
22. *Ibid.*, p. 185.
23. *Ibid.*, p. 199.
24. *Ibid.*, p. 173.
25. *Ibid.*, p. 281.
26. *Ibid.*, pp. 202 - 203.
27. *Ibid.*, pp. 139 - 40.
28. *Ibid.*, p. 164.
29. *Ibid.*, p. 165.
30. *Ibid.*, pp. 114 - 15.
31. *Ibid.*, p. 130.
32. *Ibid.*, p. 132.
33. *Ibid.*, p. 205.
34. *Ibid.*, p. 129.
35. *Ibid.*, p. 138.
36. *Ibid.*, p. 147.
37. *Ibid.*, p. 186.
38. *Ibid.*, p. 186.
39. *Ibid.*, p. 183.
40. *Ibid.*, p. 190.
41. *Ibid.*, p. 191.
42. *Ibid.*, p. 193.
43. See Pierre Trahard, *Maîtres de la sensibilité francaise au XVIIIe siècle* 4 vols, (Paris, 1933); Daniel Mornet, *La pensée francaise au XVIIIe siècle* (Paris, 1926).
44. *O. C.*, p. 178.
45. *Ibid.*, p. 81.
46. *Ibid.*, pp. 156 - 57.
47. *Ibid.*, p. 166.
48. *Ibid.*, p. 167.
49. *Ibid.*, p. 42.
50. *Ibid.*, pp. 122 - 23.
51. *Ibid.*, p. 88.

Chapter Four

1. *O. C.*, pp. 221 - 22.
2. *Ibid.*, p. 224.
3. *Ibid.*, p. 240 - 41.
4. *Ibid.*, p. 232.
5. *Ibid.*, p. 244.
6. *Ibid.*, p. 240.
7. *Ibid.*, p. 218.
8. *Ibid.*, p. 222.
9. *Ibid.*, p. 223.
10. *Ibid.*, p. 231.

11. *Ibid.*, p. 239.
12. *Ibid.*, p. 241.
13. *Ibid.*, pp. 215 - 19.
14. *Ibid.*, p. 220.
15. *Ibid.*, p. 221.
16. *Ibid.*, p. 224.
17. *Ibid.*, p. 229.
18. *Ibid.*, p. 233.
19. *Ibid.*, p. 233.
20. *Ibid.*, p. 239.
21. *Ibid.*, p. 241.

Chapter Five

1. *O. C.*, p. 251.
2. *Ibid.*, p. 265.
3. *Ibid.*, p. 280.
4. *Ibid.*, p. 285.
5. *Ibid.*, p. 286.
6. *Ibid.*, p. 253.
7. *Ibid.*, p. 254.
8. *Ibid.*, p. 255.
9. *Ibid.*, p. 257.
10. *Ibid.*, p. 263.
11. *Ibid.*, p. 279.
12. *Ibid.*, pp. 282 - 83.
13. *Ibid.*, p. 287.
14. *Ibid.*, pp. 290 - 91.
15. *Ibid.*, p. 292.
16. See Frank Bowman, *Prosper Mérimée: Heroism, Pessimism and Irony* (Berkeley, 1962); Robert C. Dale, *Poetics of Mérimée* (The Hague, 1966); Maxwell Smith, *Mérimée* (New York, 1972).
17. *O. C.*, p. 249.
18. *Ibid.*, p. 251.
19. *Ibid.*, p. 250.
20. *Ibid.*, p. 252.
21. *Ibid.*, pp. 252 - 53.
22. *Ibid.*, p. 253.
23. *Ibid.*, p. 254.
24. *Ibid.*, p. 258.
25. *Ibid.*, pp. 259 - 60.
26. *Ibid.*, pp. 262 - 63.
27. *Ibid.*, p. 263.
28. *Ibid.*, p. 263.
29. *Ibid.*, p. 264.
30. *Ibid.*, p. 268.

31. *Ibid.*, p. 281.
32. *Ibid.*, p. 259.
33. *Ibid.*, p. 260.
34. *Ibid.*, pp. 263 - 64.
35. *Ibid.*, p. 266.
36. *Ibid.*, p. 267.
37. *Ibid.*, p. 268.
38. *Ibid.*, pp. 272 - 73.
39. *Ibid.*, p. 276.
40. *Ibid.*, p. 277.
41. *Ibid.*, p. 294.

Chapter Six

1. *O. C.*, p. 321.
2. *Ibid.*, p. 323.
3. *Ibid.*, pp. 326 - 29.
4. *Ibid.*, pp. 336 - 37.
5. *Ibid.*, p. 341.
6. *Ibid.*, p. 354.
7. *Ibid.*, p. 360.
8. *Ibid.*, p. 361.
9. *Ibid.*, p. 367.
10. *Ibid.*, pp. 368 - 69.
11. *Ibid.*, pp. 370 - 71.
12. *Ibid.*, p. 301.
13. *Ibid.*, p. 317.
14. *Ibid.*, p. 322.
15. *Ibid.*, pp. 330 - 31.
16. *Ibid.*, p. 334.
17. *Ibid.*, pp. 339 - 40.
18. *Ibid.*, p. 349.
19. *Ibid.*, p. 386.
20. *Ibid.*, pp. 299 - 300.
21. *Ibid.*, p. 305.
22. *Ibid.*, p. 308.
23. *Ibid.*, p. 314.
24. *Ibid.*, p. 321.
25. *Ibid.*, p. 326.
26. *Ibid.*, pp. 328 - 29.
27. *Ibid.*, p. 335.
28. *Ibid.*, p. 344.
29. *Ibid.*, p. 307.
30. *Ibid.*, p. 312.
31. *Ibid.*, p. 327.
32. *Ibid.*, p. 353.

33. *Ibid.*, p. 318.
34. *Ibid.*, p. 356.
35. *Ibid.*, p. 359.
36. *Ibid.*, p. 364.
37. *Ibid.*, pp. 369 - 70.
38. *Ibid.*, p. 376.
39. *Ibid.*, p. 303.
40. *Ibid.*, p. 306.
41. *Ibid.*, p. 311.
42. *Ibid.*, pp. 313 - 14.
43. *Ibid.*, pp. 341 - 42.
44. *Ibid.*, pp. 345 - 46.
45. *Ibid.*, p. 349.
46. *Ibid.*, p. 363.
47. *Ibid.*, p. 378.
48. *Ibid.*, p. 379.

Chapter Seven

1. *O. I.*, I, 58 - 59.
2. *Ibid.*, p. 59.
3. *Ibid.*, p. 54.
4. *Ibid.*, pp. 61 - 62.
5. *Ibid.*, p. 69.
6. *Ibid.*, pp. 83 - 84.
7. *Ibid.*, pp. 74 - 75.
8. *Ibid.*, p. 80.
9. *Ibid.*, p. 61.
10. *Ibid.*, pp. 56 - 57.
11. *Ibid.*, p. 86.
12. *Ibid.*, p. 52.
13. Berthier, pp. 378 - 79.
14. *O. I.*, I, p. 380.
15. *Ibid.*, p. 380.
16. *Ibid.*, p. 378.
17. *Ibid.*, p. 372.
18. *Ibid.*, p. 375.
19. *Ibid.*, p. 376.
20. *O. I.*, II, 228.
21. See Count Orloff, *Fables russes de M. Kriloff* (Paris, 1825); and Alfred Bougeault, *Kryloff, sa vie et ses fables* (Paris, 1860).

Chapter Eight

1. Stendhal (Marie-Henri Beyle), *Courrier Anglais* (Paris, 1935), I, 187 - 88.

2. *Ibid.*, pp. 196, 189.

3. *Ibid.*, p. 198.

4. *Ibid.*, pp. 199 - 201.

5. *Ibid.*, pp. 189, 190.

6. Alphonse de Lamartine, *Cours familier de littérature* (Paris, 1865), XX, 12, 73.

7. *Ibid.*, XX, 13.

8. Charles Augustin Sainte-Beuve, "Le Comte Xavier de Maistre," *Revue des deux mondes"* XVIII, 2 (May 1, 1839): 302, 306, 310.

9. Anatole France, "Le Génie Latin," *Oeuvres Complètes*, (Paris, 1931), XXI, 273.

10. Henry Bordeaux, "Les Amours de Xavier de Maistre à Aoste," *Revue universelle*, XLI, 1, (April 1, 1930): 35.

11. See Charles Lombard, *French Romanticism on the Frontier* (Madrid, 1972).

12. Donald G. Mitchell, *Reveries of a Bachelor* (New York, 1850), p. 77.

13. *Ibid.*, p. 11.

14. *Ibid.*, p. 58.

15. *Ibid.*, p. 116.

16. See Rodolphe Töpffer, *Nouvelles Genevoises* (Paris, 1874).

17. See Alphonse Karr, *Voyage autour de mon jardin* (Paris, 1845).

18. Laurence Sterne, *Tristram Shandy* (Baltimore, 1967), p. 209. See Henri Glaesner, "Laurence Sterne et Xavier de Maistre," *Revue de littérature comparée*, VII, 3, (July-September, 1927): 459 - 80.

19. See Berthier, and the detailed study by E. Haumant, *La Culture française en Russie* (Paris, n. d.).

20. See Berthier, pp. 242 - 50.

Selected Bibliography

PRIMARY SOURCES

1. *Editions* (There are many excellent editions of Xavier de Maistre's individual and collected works. Owing to limitations of space only those of immediate practical use to students and researchers are listed.)

Lettres inédites a son ami Töpffer. Edited by Léon Albert Matthey. Geneva: Skira, 1945.

Lettres inédites de Xavier de Maistre à sa famille. Paris: Soye, 1902.

Oeuvres complètes du comte Xavier de Maistre. Paris: Garnier, 1862.

Oeuvres inédites de Xavier de Maistre. Edited by Eugène Réaume. 2 vols. Paris: Lemerre, 1877.

XAVIER DE MAISTRE. *Chapitre inédit d'histoire littéraire et bibliographique.* Edited by Henry Maystre. Geneva: Eggimann, 1895. Interesting letters in correspondence between Xavier de Maistre and Baron de Mareste.

2. *Translations*

A journey around my room. Translated by Henry Attwell. London: Chatto and Windus, 1883.

The leper of Aost. Translated Anonymously. Boston: Cummings, Hilliard, 1825.

Russian tales. Translated Anonymously. Philadelphia: Carey and Lea, 1826.

3. *Bibliographies*

TALVART, HECTOR, ET PLACE, JOSEPH. *Bibliographie des auteurs modernes de langue française* (1801 - 1962). Paris: Editions de la chronique des lettres françaises, 1928 - 1962.

THIEME, HUGO PAUL. *Bibliographie de la littérature française de 1800 à 1930.* Paris: Droz, 1933.

For recent studies, quarterly bibliographies of *La Revue d'histoire littéraire de la France* (RHLF) and *La Revue de la litterature comparée* may be consulted, as well as the annual bibliographies of PMLA.

SECONDARY SOURCES

BARTON, FRANCIS. *Laurence Sterne en France.* Paris: Hachette, 1911. Conscientious analysis of Sterne's influence on Xavier and other French writers.

BERTHIER, ABBÉ ALFRED. *Xavier de Maistre.* Lyon: Vitte, 1921. The best study of Xavier in French with valuable documentation and unpublished material.

GLAESNER, HENRI. "Laurence Sterne et Xavier de Maistre." *Revue de littérature comparée,* VII, 3 (July-September, 1927): 459 - 80. A fairly good comparison of the two writers.

LA FUYE, MAURICE DE. *Xavier de Maistre.* Tours: Mame, 1934. A sprightly and colorful account of chief incidents in Xavier's life.

SAINTE-BEUVE, CHARLES AUGUSTIN. "Le Comte Xavier de Maistre." *Revue des deux mondes,* XVIII 2 (May 1, 1839): 297 - 315. Sainte-Beuve's article on Xavier that caused the latter so much distress and anxiety.

UNGEWITTER, WILHELM. *Xavier de Maistre, sein Leben und seine Werke.* Berlin: Gronau, 1892. A short study with some original insights.

Index